New Harmonies

Choosing Contemporary Music for Worship

Terri Bocklund McLean

An Alban Institute Publication

Library of Congress Catalog Card Number 98-73669
ISBN 1-56699-206-0

*"By putting what is precious,
the unknown and unseen things of God (Rom. 1:20)
in common vessels (2 Cor. 4:7),
it brings them within the grasp of human minds."*

–Bernard of Clairvaux

CONTENTS

ACKNOWLEDGMENTS

There are few people who so influence a life that without their impression an individual might be altogether different. I thank and acknowledge those who were part of my Christian formation, and who called up in my heart a hunger for God and the insatiable yearning for worship that *really worships*. Handt Hanson at Prince of Peace Lutheran Church in Burnsville, Minnesota, and the Rev. Walt Kallestad at Community Church of Joy in Glendale, Arizona, are two whose love of God and worship has integrally shaped me. I was blessed to be mentored by them, and also by the Rev. Merv Thompson, as I was growing up at Prince of Peace.

Special thanks are due to many wonderful people. At my two communities of faith in Columbia and Severna Park, Maryland, there are many talented volunteers I work with, the pastors who have embraced a vision for growth and change with the Good News at its core, and all the folks in worship from week to week. I especially cherish the partnerships and friendships I have with the Rev. Bob Wallace, the Rev. Mike McQuaid, and the Rev. Ken Brown. My kids lovingly tolerated my hard work on this project, and I owe them a debt of gratitude for respecting the concept that "Mom works at home" and allowing me to make slow but steady progress. And special thanks to my husband, Steve, for all his love, support, and encouragement.

INTRODUCTION

Rows of spiral-bound songbooks line the shelves in my offices at St. John Evangelical Lutheran Church in Columbia, Maryland, and Severna Park United Methodist Church in Severna Park, Maryland, where I serve as contemporary worship team leader. My collection is an odd assortment of material, with publication dates ranging from the 1960s up to just a few months ago. All of it was written, presumably, for use in "contemporary worship." Some of it was written by professional songwriters, some by devout people of faith connected with various churches around the world and some by contemporary Christian recording artists. Some collections are published by megachurches, some by denominations at the national level, and some by huge corporations whose bottom-line goals lurk uncomfortably close to their ministry goals. Some of the material is self-published, in booklets with simple graphics.

I have often wondered how many thousands of songs I have on these shelves. I wonder what percentage of that total I have brought to my congregation to enhance its contemporary worship. I know it's a small proportion.

I've had serendipitous success in finding and using good songs for our contemporary worship services, perhaps because of my love and study of songwriting. I knew enough to know a good song when I saw one. As our services grew, we were constantly encouraged by those who remarked that the music was meaningful and inspiring, and made worship seem "alive." I knew that the credit for these accolades went first to God and then to the songs themselves, more than to the musical renditions offered by the amateur musicians who make up our praise bands. My process of picking songs from thousands of options worked for my faith communities, though it was imprecise, and resided exclusively in my head.

In meeting and talking with other contemporary worship leaders, I soon discovered that the success we enjoyed in our contemporary worship was less widespread than I would have thought. Many contemporary services, once begun, succumbed to failure, a process described by one man as "just fizzling out." From the stories of many congregational worship leaders, I eventually concluded that, after the all-important process of vision and mission, the art and science of song selection is perhaps the single most important element in contemporary worship planning, and *great songs are more important than great players and leaders*. Granted, it borders on idolatry to think that the music we choose can affect the working of the Holy Spirit, which doesn't need our music to change hearts or call people to Christ. But what we choose musically to bear the metaphors of the faith can be appealing or can be a turn-off for those who come through the doors of the church. Personal preferences are an integral part of human nature. We vote with our preferences, sometimes with our feet, and almost always with our dollars.

The Song Selection Process

Song selection has always been a satisfying task for me. I know what I'm looking for, and I always have an array of songs "on deck" and exciting ideas about how and when to use them. I realized a while ago that even though I work with a dedicated group of musicians and singers, not one of them had a clue as to how I go about finding the songs we use in worship, and how I plug them into our services. The pastors were even more distant than the musicians from this process. I had the uneasy feeling that if I were to leave my ministries or be absent for any substantial period, no one would have the slightest idea how to carry on. Such a situation is not healthy for me or the congregations. In addition, people from the congregations were bringing me song suggestions, and I had to be accountable to them for my decisions about what we used and what we didn't. I began this project to remedy the situation.

This book will not explore the validity of contemporary worship expressions, or argue the merits of the church's efforts to build bridges to contemporary culture. That development is already upon us as a full-fledged movement, now in its second generation. Instead, the book will analyze the process of song selection for contemporary and alternative worship. It will help guide any congregation in the creation and maintenance of a unique, custom-built repertoire for worship. It will present a structured, objective means for saying yes or no to a song while acknowledging and using the subjective nature of personal preference as an element in song selection. This book is a response to a crisis in church music, which author, scholar, and musician Quentin Faulkner identifies as "the lack of any widely held objective criteria that establish propriety or quality in church music."[1] Although individual preference ensures that song selection will never be an exact science, I have attempted here to organize the process into bite-size pieces to allow the worship leader to make song selection a more objective process, even a group effort. I trust that ministry happens in this process, and that the saints are equipped for a greater role in creating relevant worship for the congregation.

Tools for the Team

This project operates on certain assumptions and recommendations. The first is that it has value as a tool for congregations that are engaged in, or hope to engage in, contemporary or alternative worship. To my knowledge, this information has not been organized previously for the sole purpose of helping congregations decide which music to use and how to use it in contemporary services. It will be especially helpful to small and middle-size congregations that want to commit to a new worship style but need information, guidance, and "nuts and bolts" to get it going. It will also be helpful to congregations already involved in contemporary worship that want to fine-tune their approach and get in sync with the new "collective wisdom" on how to expand and empower their worship services.

For this methodology to be effective in a congregation, I recommend that a competent leader take on the leadership outlined in this book. I refer to the competent leader I envision as the "worship team leader." He or she is typically a lay professional whose various responsibilities ultimately manifest themselves in the execution of contemporary or alternative music of quality to enhance the congregation's worship. This person can best serve the congregation as a staff member, fully connected to the pastoral staff as a professional ministry peer, and accountable to congregational polity. The worship team leader brings a level of musical expertise and creativity to the job, as well as "people skills" and biblical literacy. He or she works toward lifting up the Gospel within the vision created by the congregation and its leaders.

This worship specialist leads, in part, by defining and opening an area of service to the congregation and inviting specific people to participate in song selection for worship. Thus is created a team, whose optimal number is between eight and twelve. A team of fewer than eight members is too small to represent the body effectively; a team of more than twelve results in an unwieldy balance for efficient decision-making.

If the worship team leader is faithful to this ministry, over time many members can be equipped for a greater role in leadership. Handt Hanson, worship team leader at Prince of Peace Lutheran Church in Burnsville, Minnesota, has said, "If I'm doing my job, there will be enough people who can do it as well as I can that it doesn't matter if I'm there at worship or not."[2] Those who are brought into the process need not be musically gifted. The greatest set of skills needed is not dazzling musicianship but a heart dedicated to the Lord, a prayerful commitment to discipleship, and a love for the work (and especially the music) of the local church. The worship team leader trains the team, using the principles set out in this book, and equips them to use the tools found in the appendixes. Applying the principles and using the tools together, the team brings the worship songs to the congregation. The antiquated top-down leadership approach is eliminated, and the work of the team brings leadership *out of* the congregation instead of aiming it *at* the congregation.

This book assumes that the congregation undertaking such a ministry project has a fully functional mission statement, which effectively guides its ministries and projects. The mission statement gives direction and focus to those involved in creating and planning contemporary or alternative worship, and they will rely on the mission statement as authority for their work and for their accountability to the congregation.

Picking the Great Songs

The annual Mid-Atlantic Song Contest sponsored by the Songwriters' Association of Washington is one of the largest songwriting contests outside of Nashville. It receives up to 2,000 entries every year. From those entries, 20 are chosen for top honors. From those 20, one is awarded the Grand Prize. Somehow, a group of people is able to decide together which songs are the best, and of the best, which one is *the* best. You can bet that no A&R (artists and repertory) rep from Nashville is going to snatch up a song ranked at number 1,156, or even number 30, for publication or pitching to a recording artist. In the church we can be just as aware of what separates greatness from mediocrity as the judges of the Mid-Atlantic Song Contest. From the thousands of songs available for use in the church today, we should use only the great ones, only the ones taking top honors. We should sing only the best we have to offer in the worship of our God. We can use the same principles as judges in a song contest, plus a few others we've borrowed from the church's history and tradition. We can look past slick advertising and professionally produced companion recordings, and make informed decisions about songs for worship, using a system that helps us identify truly well-crafted songs that accurately bear our prayers, proclamations, and praise. We can declare with authority that mediocrity is not acceptable in our churches, and we can act on that declaration objectively. As a team, we can identify great songs, and we can decide how and when to use them in our worship.

About the CD-ROM

The CD-ROM you'll find on the inside cover of this book supports the text of chapter 4. It includes examples that provide audio illustrations of the descriptions of songwriting devices. All the sample sound bites of "good" songwriting elements are taken from professional recordings in the praise-and-worship niche of the contemporary Christian music industry. To hear more of any of these songs, refer to the albums listed in appendix F. Most should be available at your local Christian bookstore. I've written and performed the samples of "bad" songwriting, and have exaggerated those qualities for emphasis. These samples are minimally produced; please take them for what they are worth as examples of what to avoid when you select songs for worship.

The CD-ROM has extended architecture and contains the work sheets found in the appendixes. You can download them onto your computer's hard drive and manipulate them for your congregation's use. Feel free to adapt them so that they are most usable for your setting. Please do not copyright your changes to these templates or distribute your changes to others for profit. Use them in the spirit in which they are offered—to enhance your congregation's worship.

CHAPTER 1

The Case for the Custom-Built Repertoire

It is only by selection, by elimination, by emphasis, that we get at the real meaning of things.

—Georgia O'Keefe[1]

Music is the most definitive expression of the contemporary or alternative worship experience. There are differences in other areas—liturgy, leadership style, the language of the faith, use of metaphors and symbols. But the music of contemporary or alternative worship is the primary feature that gives worshipers (especially nonmember or entry-level worshipers) the sense that the church is interpreting the Gospel *for their benefit.*

How do you build the body of Christ? According to Leonard Sweet, respected theological scholar and dean of the theological school at Drew University, "You build it primarily with music."[2] And whatever the music, it has to be good, if not great. Some say it must be excellent. Those who come through the doors of the church today have been steeped in a musical culture of *near-perfection*. A typical budget for the musical production of a single pop album is $150,000. That money is spent to acquire nearly perfect songs and produce them to a level of near-perfection. Despite the highly subjective nature of musical tastes, today's music consumers have come to expect that the songs they hear will have a degree of predictability and, at the same time, an element of surprise, a form and content they can understand, and production values that will be nearly perfect. In fact, the drum machines used in a great deal of pop music today have a built-in feature to add an element of "human error," so that the synthesized rhythm has just enough variation that it doesn't sound "too perfect."

Musical consumers today are listening closely, and they are

demanding. They use their purchase power to hear what they *want* to hear. Music consumers have myriad ways to choose and, in nearly every instance, the ability to turn off what they don't like. Personal preference drives a music market that can't keep up with its own efforts to make music more and more personal, to vary the choices and the delivery mechanisms. The church inherits this reality, and it has its work cut out for it.

The church has been described as the only club that exists for its nonmembers. Most contemporary or alternative worship efforts are aimed at drawing nonmembers. The Rev. Bob Wallace at St. John Evangelical Lutheran Church in Columbia, Maryland, tells a story of the congregational meeting that resulted in a "yes" vote for contemporary worship. A woman seated in the last row stood up before the vote was taken and asked, "Pastor, why are we doing all this for people who aren't even here?" He replied, "Your question shows that you understand the issue."

The church knows one thing about its members: they are generally forgiving. A choir with a few warbly sopranos or a hymn with a few wrong notes played by the organist is most often lovingly tolerated by a congregation of the entrenched faithful. But bring a group of nonmembers, church-hoppers or entry-level worshipers into the same scene, and it's a good guess that they'll never be back. Unfortunately, we can expect them to exercise the power of personal preference. If we create a service with the intention of inviting in nonmembers, we must know something about their preferences and offer great songs in sync with those preferences. Musicians must render those songs well. Otherwise, we miss the mark, and we shouldn't be surprised when our contemporary or alternative services "just fizzle out."

Using great songs and rendering them well are the outward manifestations of some basic principles. First, good songs are valuable as a tool for outreach-oriented worship. The Rev. Tim Wright, author of *Community of Joy,* states that "quality-conscious congregations will attract quality-conscious consumers."[3] This idea makes some of us a little nervous, especially when we "members" know that it's the Holy Spirit who attracts people to Christ. Yet the church has to work within the confines of an imperfect world seated squarely in post-Christendom, and it is faced with all the quirks of human nature, right down to "If it's boring or bad, it's not worth my time." Wright believes that reaching the nonmember world with the Gospel requires the church to respond to consumer values if it is to be attractive and inviting. He boldly states that if the music sounds like junk, guests will proceed to the next assumption: that the church is junk. Nonmembers and entry-level Christians assume that the absence of high-quality music indicates that the church doesn't have its act together.[4]

Paul Westermeyer, a musician, teacher, and author, has said, "The incarnation has led the church to sing its faith in the musical language of the people who embrace its message."[5] In his view, "A large part of the church musician's vocation is to care for the gift of music responsibly. This means making judgments about what music is used and how it is used . . . the church musician's vocation is to do this for the local assembly, so that the congregations in their worship do not waste their time on what is not worth their while or become ensnared by what is misused."[6] In making these decisions, it is essential to consider the congregation, from the perspective not only of who they are, but also of what they can sing. "What is important here is not style, but what people can sing. The worshiping assembly can do what human beings without rehearsal can do—sing simple musical structures in an idiom they understand, structures that make logical musical sense so that they can be remembered easily enough for singing among normal people . . . this requires teaching and has to bear some relation to a musical language that is in the ear of the people."[7] This point is critical in music selection. For instance, true worship would not be facilitated for a congregation of retirees if the music chosen were hard rock or rap with "Jesus lyrics." It would most likely result in irate rather than inspired worshipers. The worship team leader is responsible for knowing what musical language is in the ears of the people, and then finding music for the congregation whose lyrics accurately bear the Gospel and the message of the sacraments.

The Expanding Repertoire

Contemporary Christian Music magazine describes the Christian music market as "niche-driven." One of the areas of greatest success (in business terms) is contemporary music for worship, the "praise-and-worship" niche. The industry is producing more music for worship than ever before, and churches are lapping it up. Many major publishing houses offer subscription services, so that the newest, hottest music is sent every few weeks in whatever form works best for convenient review—CD, cassette, or lead sheets (print music with melody line and guitar chords). The worship team leader has somehow to sort through it all while staying within budget and remaining familiar enough with all the resources to know what's current and available—no small task, especially when the worship team leader can't just find a few hundred songs that work and stick with them for 15 years or so.

The worship team leader, as chief keeper of the worship repertoire, must constantly add new songs and put others "out to pasture" to keep the worship truly contemporary. Unless the repertoire changes, a contemporary or alternative worship community will begin to settle into its own unique "tradition." Leaders can work against this phenomenon by employing a vital ministry of song search and selection, bringing a fresh flow of new music into the worship regularly.

It is chiefly the responsibility of the worship team leader to devise a methodology and to invite others into a ministry team for song selection. This project is designed to help the worship team leader and the song-selection team create and use a system for applying their own seal of approval to contemporary and alternative worship music. It is a method that will be marked, as professor and author Gordon Lathrop encourages, "by both welcome and critique, by the open gate and the warning ('Nothing unclean may enter here!' [Rev. 21:27]), by yes and no."[8]

This project, then, is about finding great songs and using them appropriately in worship. It is an important behind-the-scenes facet of the high-quality musical experience the church should create (especially if it wants to invite nonmembers) as it undertakes any alternative to traditional worship. It will describe how to make sure the contemporary songs chosen as alternatives to traditional hymnody are great ones, and how and when to use them in the worship of the triune God.

The Four-Filter Process of Song Evaluation

Like a good cup of coffee, the songs for worship are "filtered"—filtered through a specific set of criteria. Four filters comprise this process—assessing theology, matching our music to our mission, evaluating the songwriting, and plugging our music into our worship. Some songs will not make it past the first filter because of inadequate theological content. Some will be eliminated in the second filter because they aren't a good match for the musical mission of a specific service in a specific congregation. The third filter evaluates songwriting elements. Songs that pass through each of these three filters can be considered usable in worship, and will then be filtered through a song-use process, which defines how and when the song is best used in worship. This system also rates the passing songs on a point scale, so that the songs receiving a high score can be understood to be especially strong, can be used with great confidence and authority, and can be considered for longer-term use in worship (see figure 1).

During the Christmas season of the Gulf War, I sang "Laudamus Te" from Vivaldi's *Gloria* in the church we were then attending. After the service, my young daughter Britt was obviously disturbed about something. She asked me, "Mommy, why did you sing that song about Saddam Hussein?" My reply was total confusion. "What? What are you talking about?" Then she sang it back to me, the same great melodic motif of "Laudamus Te," do mi, fa, sol. . . "Sa-ddam Hu-ssein . . ." This simple story illustrates an important point. People listen from their own context of familiarity. Britt's context was the nightly TV news stories of the siege of Baghdad. The use of Latin in the song had her searching her "context bank" for something that made sense. She made sense of it all right, but her assumption was completely incorrect. Our contemporary and alternative music for worship has to present the Gospel correctly *and* connect with the context banks of those who are worshiping and those who we hope will be worshiping. The filters in this project can help ensure our success.

Four Filter Process of Song Selection

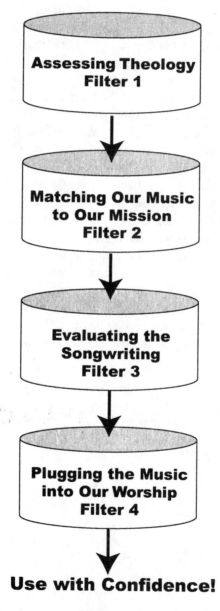

Figure 1

CHAPTER 2

Filter One:
Assessing Theology

Cultural patterns of all sorts. . . are welcome here. But they are not welcome to take the place of the Lamb. They are not welcome to obscure the gift of Christ in the Scripture read and preached, in the water used in his name, and in the thanksgiving meal.

–Gordon Lathrop[1]

Lyric content is the single most important factor in determining which songs we use in worship. We can agree to use less-than-musically-perfect songs, and those that are a less-than-perfect match to our mission. There are no perfect songs, and very few perfect mission matches. These less-than-perfect offerings do not compromise the integrity of worship. We cannot, however, agree to use songs that speak anything less than the Gospel truth. The guiding principle is this: If a song for worship does not bear the truth or an accurate metaphor of the truth, it is simply not appropriate for Christian worship. It may be appropriate for other uses, even uses that point toward God and a relationship with Christ. But without a core of Gospel truth, a song must be regarded as antagonistic to the goals of Christian worship. Author, musician, and lecturer Marva Dawn puts it this way: "No matter how musically wonderful, pieces must be rejected if the text is theologically inadequate."[2]

If one listens first to a "Top 40" radio station (popular hits) and then flips to a "CCM" (contemporary Christian music) station, it certainly will not be the music that "gives away" what's going on in the song and who or what it is about. Musically, the songs of Christian pop and rock charts are indistinguishable from their mainstream counterparts. Production and artistry are equally professional, and the contemporary Christian music of today seeks not only to emulate the musical style of the mainstream but also to forge progressive musical paths in the industry and its market. John Fischer, author of the monthly column "Consider This" in *CCM* magazine, writes in the March 1998 issue, "I find new Christian groups to be more creative than what the general market is producing right now. This is a time of great opportunity for Christian music—a time I believe God has prepared." What distinguishes the CCM song from the Top 40 hit is the lyric. If music itself functions only as the vessel of our faith, then the lyrics alone are the water of life. They bear the task of telling a part of the story that encourages our faith. In contemporary Christian music, and especially in the market niche of music for the church's worship, that story must be told accurately, it must be central, and it must be discernible.

The Importance of Music as Truth-Bearer

People assume that the music they hear in "the world" or the music they sing in worship bears the truth and accentuates what is important. We as a culture have assigned music the important task of bearing the truths we hold dear, and of celebrating that which is important and central to many. Music is the exclamation point of festival and ceremony. Consider the Super Bowl halftime show, the Thanksgiving Day parade, the bride's wedding procession—and imagine these events without music. Even my local Safeway understands this phenomenon; the store had a strolling violinist at its grand opening. I bumped into him in the frozen-foods aisle! Music has been endowed with the power to heighten celebration and ceremony, and to promote and highlight truth. This fact is the first to keep in mind as we consider why the good news borne out in the congregation's song must be accurate. A worship song with a catchy tune and a clever hook that doesn't tell the truth is detrimental to the worship of the people, because the message embedded in song is assumed by most, quite indiscriminately, to be important and correct. Songs have the ability to become "stuck" in one's head. Who hasn't been tormented by a song that refuses to leave one's consciousness, by lyrics that ride piggyback into one's thoughts along with a persistent tune to which they're wed? If a song, by its musical avenues, is able to be resurrected and embedded in a continuous play loop in one's conscious thinking, the lyrics can potentially work deep into our minds. A song bearing inaccuracies about the nature of

God or the Good News has enormous potential to affect the discipleship process adversely.

I recently heard on Christian radio a song about forgiveness that would have been perfectly usable in my context until the lyrics took a sharp turn toward works righteousness: "How can He forgive you if you don't first forgive?" While this idea pulled out of context might be biblically defensible and isn't necessarily "wrong," the single idea placed against the heart of the biblical story is incomplete. It fails to offer the kind of grace Christ died to give. Our human natures have pegged us as grudge-bearers and scorekeepers, imperfect in the art of forgiveness. If we are believers, we already know that about ourselves, and we're trying hard to be Christlike in how we forgive. Yet we know that our salvation rests on our faith, not on the perfection of our ability to forgive. If we were unbelievers, we would hear this lyric and simply give up. "It's impossible—the Jesus thing is not for me!"

Theological Economy of Worship

In worship planning, we strive for words and actions with theological economy: What we say, sing, and do speaks chiefly of the nature of God and the Good News of Jesus Christ. Robin Leaver, professor of music at Trinity College in England as well as an author and scholar, asserts quite simply, "Christians are to come to terms with the word of Christ and then proclaim it through music."[3] If our words and actions do not speak of these things specifically, we must ask ourselves what exactly *is* being spoken of. Marva Dawn describes a worship song in which the word "I" appears 28 times. She proposes that the song is not about God at all; it is about "me." A great deal of new worship music is really about "me," and this fact is well hidden under other God-talk. At first glance, these are nice songs about my commitment to God. They witness to my faith. They say what I will do. Upon closer examination, however, they may not proclaim anything about God but rather proclaim a great deal about me. They don't serve as praise, as they are not directed toward God and never directly address God. Although the lyrics may be obviously God-related, they are people-centered. Handt Hanson is quick to point out that in a responsible theological economy, good worship music should be the other way around—God-centered and people-related. This distinction may seem to be hairsplitting, but it is one crucial consideration in the task of choosing what's best for the church's worship. Scott Weidler, associate director for worship and music for the Evangelical Lutheran Church in America, further describes this subtlety in comparing two songs, "I Have Decided to Follow Jesus" and "I Want Jesus to Walk With Me." Here a fine line distinguishes the theologies of the songs. Decision theology (God meets us through our decision to accept Christ) is represented in "I Have Decided to Follow Jesus," while the similarly titled "I Want Jesus to Walk With Me" represents a theology of the cross (God meets us through Jesus' death on the cross and subsequent resurrection).[4] Certainly one is more appropriate than the other for a given church, depending on the congregation's history, beliefs, and denominational ties. What is required is discernment—a careful, faithful look at the lyric, asking simply, "Is this the truth as we have interpreted it?" Westermeyer adds, "We must specifically reject songs that add our efforts to God's saving work. Songs that stress our searching for God or our success at finding him ignore the total inability of our sinful selves to want or to find God, and miss the immense searching of God's gracious love."[5]

The Truth Is the Gospel

The songs of worship must also place the Good News and this God-centered quality discernibly at the fore. Even amid metaphorical language, the message should be unmistakably *the* unique Good News of Jesus Christ, not some other genre of good news or some other ultimate truth. According to Leaver, this proclamatory nature of the music of worship "guards against anthropocentric worship which wallows in nontheological sentimentality and a kind of church music which tells us only about what we already know and does not challenge us with the dynamic reality of God's word."[6] Many other institutions are well-equipped for the task of promoting other truths. The church's business is not to promote truths advocated elsewhere; its primary task is to spread its own unique, exclusive truth, unavailable in any other venue, that "God so loved the world that he gave his one and only Son, that whoever believes in him shall not perish but have eternal life"(John 3:16, NIV). Sally Morgenthaler, author of *Worship Evangelism*, puts it this way: "Technique is not the power for salvation. Entertainment is not the power for salvation. Psychology is not the power for salvation. 'How-To' Christianity is not the power for salvation. The Gospel is the power for salvation, and all of our technique, entertainment, psychology, and 'how-to' principles need to serve the Gospel."[7] If the church takes on the responsibility of promoting other truths (intentionally or unintentionally), it will do so less effectively than the world will, and it will usurp the rightful center of our worship. Worship songs that are vague about the source of salvation or who "holds the keys" must be carefully evaluated for their adequacy as truth-bearers of the Christian faith.

Recognizing and Embracing Theology in Lyric Content

To evaluate the theological content and relative truth of a song lyric effectively, it is important first to separate the lyric from all other aspects of the song. Simply reading through the lyrics, disregarding all other features of the song, and evaluating them by use of the "Assessing Theology Worksheet" (see appendix A) is all that is required. This is the responsibility of the worship team leader, whose job it is to connect the lyric with other previously established sources of theological truth embraced by the congregation or denomination.

Leaver encourages the worship team leader to serve as a liturgical theologian. "The musician who leads the music of the church at worship . . . is someone who is aware of the theological functions of music within the worship of the people of God."[8] The worship team leader uses specific sources of truth to establish authority for the theological filter. The Bible and denominational confessional, theological, liturgical, or historical documents, along with some ecumenical documents, such as *Baptism, Eucharist and Ministry* (Geneva: World Council of Churches, 1982), can provide just and appropriate authority for theological truth, along with interpretive insights that make up the "leading edge" of some current theological dialogue.

For each worship community, a few "pet" theologies will likely shape its identity. From among the riches of the current repertoire of contemporary worship music, songs can be chosen that are, at best, in agreement with these favored theologies and, at worst, not in direct conflict. The concept of grace is the hallmark theology of the Protestant denominations. As of summer 1998, even Roman Catholics have acknowledged an "official" embrace of this concept of our justification.

This bedrock understanding is a good place to start in shaping any repertoire. In the concept of justification, humans are seen as meriting salvation by no other means than by the goodness of God's grace extended toward humanity by and through the saving act of Christ on the cross. Faith in the human heart apprehends this gift of salvation. Our works, our strivings toward God, our lifestyle—none of these things merits the good gift of grace we have been given. To that end, Leaver declares that "Music in worship is the language of faith, the response of the redeemed to the grace of God."[9] An Adventist church might boost its repertoire with songs that reflect the glory of God and the promise of Christ's coming again. A United Methodist congregation might want a good percentage of its repertoire to celebrate the gift of salvation and the responsibility that salvation bears out in social justice and good works. A Lutheran community of faith heartily embraces baptism and Eucharist as central to its worship identity and Christian identity. Songs affirming that belief will be important in its repertoire.

Leaver identifies the doctrine of the Trinity as an essential piece of the framework of Christian theology. "It is therefore the framework for worship and music in worship as the people of God assemble together to rejoice at salvation in Christ by using the natural gifts endowed by the Father and the sanctified gifts bestowed by the Spirit."[10] Finally, Christian theology is a theology of the cross. It is a system of understanding our salvation based on the brokenness of the human condition and our need for a Saviour, and on the sufficiency of the life, death, and resurrection of that Saviour, who is Jesus Christ, for the salvation of many. It is from the cross that all mercy, grace, and salvation flow. It is the work of Christ on the cross that presents us clean and unstained before God, and the work of the Holy Spirit that changes us, shapes us, and makes us new. For our worship, we can choose songs that promote these theologies. Consider the titles of these contemporary songs for worship: "Only By Grace," "In the Water," "Poured Out and Broken," "Amazing Love." By the titles alone, we can hear the ring of these theologies.

Embracing these theologies inevitably means that we are connected to some part of the past, to the history of how we think about our faith and the words we choose to speak about it. Embracing this specific set of theologies provides the contemporary church with a point of convergence where it meets the church of all of our yesterdays since the cross. Embracing this set of theologies and employing them intentionally in our songs, words, and actions of worship keeps the contemporary church accountable to the heart and soul of the Christian faith.

Moreover, Leaver asserts that "the relationship between music and theology preserves the character of Christian worship: theology prevents music from assuming an independent role in the worship of the church."[11] Our efforts to make something new in worship are worthy only when they remain true, and when we acknowledge that the truth has a reference point in history that has moved steadily toward us in a train of days and years, movements and reformations, and conversations and confrontations. Further, we are oriented to an event that forever changed the course of history and the future of humankind, and that event lay in the deep and wide waters of ancient Israelite worship practices, writings, and lifestyles. We are oriented by our Bible to the faith experience of an ancient people who set down in words their devotion to God even before the time of Moses. We are oriented by the words of the prophets to a description of a Messiah, a hoped-for Saviour who would restore the kingdom. We are oriented by the work of the reformers to an interpretation of the Gospel truths that salvation is for all and that faith is the only means by which it is apprehended.

As seductive as it may seem to fashion our worship around our needs and our immediate context, regarding the history of the church as irrelevant, what ultimately happens in such a setting is not worship of the God who is deserving of our thanks and praise, but worship of ourselves, held hostage by our culture, our context, and our preferences. We cannot and should not reinvent the wheel.

Worship needs to be *about Jesus Christ*. This reality comes with certain risks. The risks are in the call to connect our worship unabashedly, unswervingly, and intentionally at every possible level to the person and work of Jesus Christ, the goodness of God, and the power of the Holy Spirit. A powerful tendency today pulls believers to respond to the popular and attractive New Age movement, which advocates a wide, rather nondescript path toward the light, in which being "spiritual" is far more useful than being "religious" or, even more narrowly, being "Christian." The success and momentum of the New Age movement tugs powerfully at the methods of evangelical outreach that might turn hearts toward worship of the triune God. Christians feel an urge to render the message of Christ so palatable, so appealing, and so unobtrusive that those hearing it for the first time might draw the conclusion that this faith is about ease and comfort, and all that is required is "tuning in," as to a favorite television show.

Yet we must remember that since the day of Christ himself, the message of the Gospel was radical and countercultural. Discipleship required and still requires leaving everything and simply following Christ. Even when we package this message in a culturally relevant context, it is no less radical and countercultural today. Handt Hanson suggests that we must find a "radical middle where we can learn to speak each other's language,"[12] and in this radical middle the message of the Gospel, whole and intact, bridges the distance to popular culture without being accommodated to it. Gordon Lathrop, who has contributed a wealth of scholarly work in this regard, suggests that we need to use what culture has to offer us, that "just as we always need local words to be able to speak, we will always need something of local metaphors simply to gather,"[13] and what is required is to "break them" to the purposes of the Gospel, as a horse is broken to the purposes of its owner.[14] Sally Morgenthaler urges us to take the best of what popular culture has to offer, not the junk, and to move from there toward a "worship that takes the new and makes it true; and takes the old and makes it new."[15]

Reed Arvin, one of contemporary Christian music's most successful and well-respected producers, calls upon writers of Christian music to see their task in a new light. Gone are the days, he says, when we could take direct quotes of Scripture and embed them in a catchy tune. He believes that most people simply "don't have ears" for that kind of message anymore.[16] Gone are the days when we can write a slew of one-emotion songs aimed at the happy Christian, or publish a collection of peppy, upbeat songs for the cheerleading-for-God Christian. The craft of songwriting for worship is literally "dying for something different." It is incumbent upon the writers of worship music to craft their songs with the depth and breadth of the truths of the faith and of human experience. It is essential to write songs to say these things in new ways, so that the truth is spoken (as Morgenthaler describes) with *our* turn of a phrase, *our* metaphors, applied meaningfully to *our* particular struggles and triumphs in life and in faith.

This first filter concerns itself with the centrality of the truth, realizing full well that much is happening in the worship songs pitched to local churches today. What *must* be going on is, first and foremost, the truth of the Gospel. With as many different spins on the truth as there are denominations, it is up to the local church to make certain that the brand of truth in the songs we sing in worship matches the one we are preaching to our members and visitors.

Using the Assessing Theology Filter

It is the worship team leader's job to employ the "Assessing Theology" filter, using the worksheet in appendix A, which is annotated below. The worship team leader should be biblically literate and aware of the basic tenets of the Scriptures, as well as the gist of the congregation's confessional perspective.

The most useful tool a worship team leader can rely on for this filter is an exhaustive biblical concordance, available in print or as a computer software program. A concordance helps the worship team leader connect themes, key words, and ideas in songs to the written Word, which is the ultimate resource for truth. The pastor is an essential resource in this filter as well, helping to orient and guide the worship team leader through what might be murky theological waters.

The "Assessing Theology" filter is a three-step process based on a point system. After reading the lyrics of a song aloud, the worship team leader identifies key words and any theological "cons" in the lyrics. Presence of a "con" immediately fails a song. Theological "cons"are images or statements contrary to biblical truth; images or statements contrary to your denomination's confessional basis; questionable interpretations of Scripture; Scriptures linked to incompatible images; works righteousness; and absence of Christian content.

The second step of the filter is to identify theological "pros" in the lyrics. Each "pro" receives five points. Theological "pros" are as follows: references and images rooted in Scripture (identified by lifting key words, images, and ideas from the lyric and, using a Concordance, locating biblical texts that support the lyric); baptismal references, images, or invitations; eucharistic references, images, or invitations; references to justification by faith through grace; references to the triune nature of God; references to Christ's work on the cross; references to our salvation through Christ's work on the cross; and acknowledgment of our brokenness and need for a Saviour. Blank spaces are offered for insertion of other theological "pros" that your congregation may want to embrace as it shapes its custom repertoire.

Another important "pro" is that the song is sung from the perspective of the assembly, not the individual. When the song uses "we" and "us" in the lyric (as opposed to "I" and "me"), it creates the important and necessary horizontal axis of the worship experience. A disproportionate number of songs written for contemporary worship promote an individualism detrimental to the understanding that worship is a public event, a community-based encounter with God. It is not just a vertical experience of "Jesus and me." Martin Seltz, editor of congregational song at Augsburg Fortress Publishers, says, "It seems obvious, but the mark of a good song for . . . worship is that it is the song of the assembly."[17] A song written from the perspective of the congregation also receives five points.

Two nonfailing "cons" are identified in addition to those mentioned above. Songs with archaic language and songs with "exclusive" language should be regarded as containing theological "cons." Archaic language such as "thee," "thou," and "thy" is simply not used in conversation today and speaks of a bygone era. These words are not even included in the spell-checker of my state-of-the-art word-processing software. Use of archaic language may convey to visitors and entry-level worshipers that the way we speak to or about God has not evolved since the time of King James. Similarly, 20 years have elapsed since we generally acknowledged that "mankind" is not an appropriate expression for "all of us." There is simply no excuse for using noninclusive language today. However, songs with archaic and noninclusive language can sometimes be successfully altered without compromising a song's integrity. For instance, the very popular Michael W. Smith and Amy Grant song "Thy Word" could be sung as "Your Word" without taking the song too far from the composers' intentions. There is no real change in meaning, no rhythmic or melodic interruption, and no resyllabification. Though it seems a small, insignificant change, the publisher should be contacted directly to request permission for even small changes to any copyrighted lyric. The alteration of "all mankind" to "all people" and similar changes to achieve inclusive language should also be checked out with the publisher.

Two current "hot buttons" define the leading edge of the "Assessing Theology" filter. The first is the use of male pronouns for God. The second is a cross-cultural or multicultural awareness. If a song uses no male pronouns for God, it is given ten additional points. Although many mainline denominations have worked hard to rein in the concept of God's maleness in their print materials and in the seminaries, the question of male pronouns for God is still wide open among the folks. Just bring up the topic at a church supper and see what happens. As a church, we are not ready to abandon these words for God, but we should be aware of widening our images of who God is and how we describe God. Martin Seltz indicates that we are now in the dawn of at least attempting to avoid male pronouns. He believes the use of "Lord" will stay, but we should avoid the continual "piling up" of male imagery in representing God. If we're going to go one way or the other, we should err on the side of pointing to God without the suggestion of maleness. Poetic creativity will assist us in finding ways of referring to God other than in male pronouns.[18]

Second, more than ever, we live in a global community. Using only music that reminds us of ourselves denies the existence of our brothers and sisters across the world and their unique contributions to the richness of culturally and ethnically rooted worship expressions. We are connected as a family, even "members of each other" (Ephes. 4:25), and therefore it is important to use each other's songs, or at least to acknowledge that we are connected to a global Christian family in our worship. "World music" is steadily (and delightfully) infiltrating our once-exclusive realm of European-derived musical forms and sounds. More and more frequently, we hear the unfamiliar erupting in the midst of the familiar. Even our commercials feature music from around the globe. Tuvan throat singing, Native American flute, and Tibetan yak bells remind us that it's a small, small world. A worship song with lyrics that connect us to other Christians in other places, specifically or generically, receives ten extra points.

All around Your throne,
We come from every language and nation,
Making Your glories known,
Lifting aloud our song of salvation,
All around Your throne!

The point system in this filter helps us to know a song that bears the truth when we see one. A song earning at least ten points in the "pros" column should be considered as passing. Songs with higher scores can be regarded as valuable to the worship context, and these can be used with utmost confidence (if they also pass the second and third filters) to convey the truth of the Gospel to those who will gather to worship.

CHAPTER 3

FILTER TWO:
Matching Our Music
to Our Mission

It's easy to say "no!" when there's a deeper "yes!" burning inside.

—Stephen Covey[1]

Perhaps nothing so defines a church eager for the 21st century as its vision. Vision is the difference between a church ducking the demands of the future and the changes ahead, and a church driven by what it perceives the Lord has called it to do, eagerly preparing for its next step toward that calling. Vision is the difference between a church looking inward at its problems and disabilities and a church looking outward with compassion on the surrounding community. Vision is the difference between a church that faces closing down in the next 20 years unless something miraculous happens and a church that will, in that same time, enthusiastically expand its ministries and disciple-making. When the inevitable words "We've never done it that way before" make their reprise, vision is the difference between a church that responds with a shrug and a "Let's not go there," and a church that says, "Yes, well then, how can we make it work?"

There are a host of high-powered consultants promoting their concepts of vision and mission to individuals, organizations, and the church. All basically echo what the writer of Proverbs contended: "Where there is no vision, the people are unrestrained" (Prov. 29:18, NAS). Stephen Covey takes the assertion one step further, stating that vision is "the primary motivation of human action. . . . It's the ability to see beyond our present reality, to create, to invent what does not yet exist, to become what we not yet are. It gives us capacity to live out our imagination instead of our memory."[2] He urges the importance of incorporating vision into a specific mission statement that serves the vision—that which the congregation perceives God is calling it to do. At St. John Evangelical Lutheran Church in Columbia, Maryland (and probably at your church), the mission statement came into being before the contemporary worship service; yet it still provides guidance for the work of the song-selection team. St. John's mission statement declares:

> The community of faith gathered at St. John Evangelical Lutheran Church exists to spread the Word of God and to nurture persons in the Word of God.

It is followed by the vision statement:

We will create places of welcome where persons can:

Seek answers to the pressing problems of life;
Cultivate a relationship with Jesus Christ and other people;
Celebrate the gift of new life; and
Serve the human hurts and hopes in our midst.

The mission statement defines for the congregation the reason for its existence; it states the vision in terms of broad ministry goals. The clarity offered by such a tool is critical; it affects everything else—the goals we set, the decisions we make, the expectations we have and the way we spend our time.[3] For the church, a mission statement very simply shapes what we do in our ministries and in our worship, and always serves the overall vision of the congregation. It acts as a constant reminder of what's important, and helps us to avoid the time and energy vampires that can effectively sidetrack our goals and dreams. Covey explains, "Teams and organizations with a strong sense of mission significantly outperform those without the strength of vision."[4] Here it is important to understand that the goal of the individual church is not to outperform other churches in the community (although that might be a result), but rather to be as faithful and effective as possible in lifting up the Gospel and introducing people to and equipping them for a vital relationship with Christ.

From the congregational mission statement, we create a two-tiered music mission statement that connects with the congregational vision. Beginning with a preamble, "We will shape our repertoire with songs that . . . ," the team defines the thematic qualities that it will use to endorse songs for worship. St. John could state the first tier for its music mission statement this way:

We will shape our repertoire with songs that:

- Express the Word and its saving message for all people, and its special promise for the individual.
- Acknowledge our human condition and provide answers to our problems.
- Have a vertical and/or a horizontal feature; they speak of a relationship to Christ, and/or a relationship to other people.
- Have a quality of celebration, that speak of our gifts in Christ and the blessings we live out in the promise of abundant life with our Savior.
- Orient us to our call to serve others around us.

These statements, drawn from the congregational mission statement, serve as the first tier of the music mission statement (see fig. 2).

Music Mission Statement:
A Double Filter Process

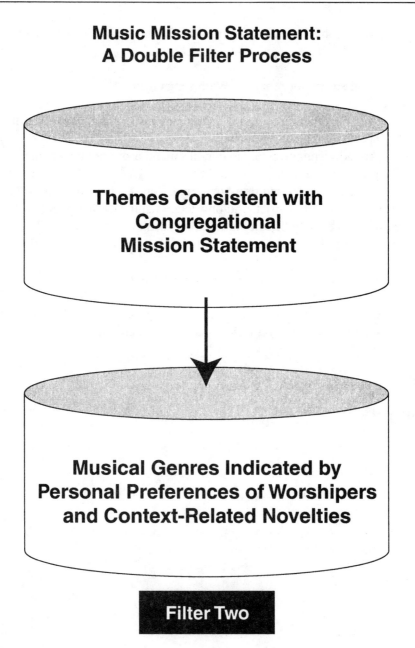

Figure 2

They give us reasons to say yes or no to a song that go far beyond "because I like it" or "because I don't." The focus of the music mission statement helps to weed out songs that contain inadequate theology and mediocre songwriting. Primarily, it helps give the song-selection team an objective set of standards for considering what it accepts for its worship. In the second tier, it identifies a group of musical styles that will work for a given faith community. It helps the team build a custom repertoire of songs that intentionally and consistently say what is important and vital to say about our God and about our faith, instead of saying what is (at best) not worth saying and (at worst) just plain incorrect, tangential to our mission, or counterproductive. It results in responsible and faithful stewardship of the most powerful and mysterious medium of worship—music.

Connecting to Personal Preferences

The next step in creating a music mission statement brings the plethora of musical genres and personal preferences into play, and objectively claims a few that will work best in a given congregation. This forms the second tier of the music mission statement. A few basic principles drive this step. First, the contemporary and alternative worship music we choose serves two populations. It serves those of us who are already here, worshiping, asking questions, and living out a faith walk with Christ. It also serves those who haven't yet come through the doors of the church, people who are most likely living within a five-mile radius of our building. Second, for a variety of reasons, it is unwise to expect that our church will be able to use *all* musical genres in worship before the Eschaton. The first reason was defined earlier: *The church must respond to consumer values to be attractive and inviting.* People don't like *all* music. People like *some* music. Typically, people in a community have some agreement on what kind of music they like best. The demographics of personal preference drive what is stocked at the local music store, and what is played on the most successful radio stations. The largest section at a music store in the Mall of America in suburban Minneapolis will likely be different from the one in downtown Atlanta, which will differ from the one in Bozeman, Montana. The preferences of those attending worship and those we hope will attend worship define, in large part, which *few* genres will be most used in a given congregation.

Determining specific preferences in your community is easily done by asking a few simple questions of the right people in the right places. The method need not be strictly scientific. It is not necessary to get caught up in complicated strategies or statistics.

The questions:
  1. What kind of music do you like best?
  2. Who are your favorite artists or bands?
  3. What are your presets on your car stereo?

The people:
  1. Those in the community of faith.
  2. Those in the community surrounding the community of faith.

The format for acquiring the information may be accomplished in a simple survey, asked of a sampling of people. The song-selection ministry team can gather information from members of the congregation on a Sunday morning or at a well-attended church event. The team can gather information from the community surrounding the church by surveying people as they enter the local grocery store or the corner convenience mart, as they tank up at the local gas station, or as they watch the soccer game at the elementary school up the street. Anywhere "the community" comes and goes is a good place to ask the questions. The numbers of people surveyed is relatively unimportant, so long as the team is satisfied that it has a reliable sampling from the communities (see appendix B).

The worship team leader can then collate the information, identifying three musical genres most often named as favorites (represented by favorite artists or styles and by the genres played on favorite radio stations) by those in the communities surveyed. The team then creates language to incorporate the selected genres into its music mission statement. St. John identified soft rock, country, and the "unplugged" sound of contemporary acoustic as definitive of the musical mission; thus the following constitutes the secondary tier of the music mission statement: "We will shape our repertoire with songs that can be presented to the congregation in the musical genres of soft rock, country, and contemporary acoustic" (see fig. 2).

The Role and Importance of Novelty

A word about *novelty* is needed at this point. Note that the sentence above says, "We will shape our repertoire" and not "We will sing these kinds of songs to the exclusion of all others." Certainly, other kinds of songs can and should be considered for use by the congregation, and some songs outside the musical genres selected *will* enhance the worship of the people. These songs can be considered as novelties. They serve to add an element of variety and cross-cultural awareness to the worship and often an element of fun. In considering a song to be used as a novelty, it is important first to tag it as a potential novelty song, identifying the genre that puts it outside the preference zone defined by the music mission statement. Second, it becomes especially important to evaluate such songs using the processes described in chapters two, four, and five. They must also connect to the principles described in chapter seven, considering especially the limitations of the band's capabilities (e.g., what the musicians in the band can play, and play well). A band made up of people whose musical experience is limited to country and rock will not go swiftly into an excellent execution of a complex jazz piece.

Using the Music Mission Statement

Making the music mission statement useful on an ongoing basis requires cooperation and delegation of duties among the worship team leader and the team. Not everyone need be involved in every aspect of song selection, and the first step is solely the worship team leader's responsibility. He or she is the person responsible for staying abreast of what is available in the worship music market. Mailings from publishing houses announcing new material will be directed to him or her. The worship team leader is presumably "tuning in" frequently to some current source of Christian music, whether it be radio, television, or the internet. These media sources provide a "full-color" sampling of what's new and what's available as opposed to the strictly black-and-white presentation of print music. I encourage worship team leaders to go to their local Christian bookstore from time to time for an afternoon of sample listening. Most Christian bookstores have a listening station and a rack of "demos" that include worship music releases. *Worship Leader* magazine's feature "Song-Discovery" is an excellent and affordable resource for those who don't have easy access to a Christian bookstore. For those on-line and those in rural areas, the computer provides terrific "cyber" listening alternatives. Many web sites offer listening opportunities, and surfing for worship music can be fun and efficient. Use your favorite search engine and key in "praise & worship" for a peek at the vast landscape of information available. Exercises in listening bear much fruit in providing ideas and resources to the worship team leader, and do so without an investment of precious church funds.

From these and a variety of other resources, the worship team leader decides what to purchase for the congregation. From the music purchases made, the leader reviews the songs, using the music mission statement as a pretest for deciding which songs should be presented to the team for further consideration. Songs either pass or fail this filter, there being no "middle ground" (see fig. 3).

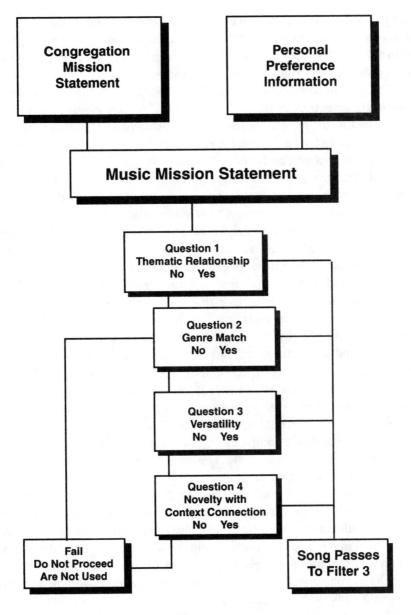

Figure 3

Using the worksheet in appendix C, the worship team leader asks up to four questions of a song to pass or fail it. The worship team leader must give a yes to both the first and second tiers of the music mission statement to move the song to the next filter for consideration.

The first question relates to the thematic content defined in the music mission statement. *Does the lyric content of this song relate to any of the themes endorsed by the music mission statement?* If your mission statement is broad, as most are, the majority of songs will pass this step of the process with a yes, and proceed to the next question. Those evaluated as *not* relating strongly to the congregation's mission statement are tagged as an inadequate mission match, fail at this point of the evaluation, and proceed no further. For instance, in relation to St. John's music mission statement above, "Making War in the Heavenlies" would fail, because even the title makes clear that the song's content is not connected to any theme endorsed by the music mission statement.

The second question focuses on genre. *Is this song composed in a musical genre that is compatible with any identified by our music mission statement?* As an experienced musician, the worship team leader should be able to identify the style or genre of most songs by their rhythmic, harmonic, and melodic elements. Companion recordings can also be helpful in identifying musical genre. If the answer to the question is yes, the song is passed on to the next filter. If no, the song proceeds to the next question in this filter. A notation to this effect is made on the work sheet (see appendix C), where the worship team leader keeps a permanent and easy reference trail of a song's evaluation at this entry level.

Muzak is famous for its "elevator music" remixes. With a remix—a recasting of the musical arrangement—a successful song in one market or genre is repackaged for a different market. Muzak isn't alone; remixing is done frequently in the music industry to enhance a great song's potential for profit. Often a major hit tune from pop radio is put through the remix process and given a "dance music" spin for use in clubs, or a Muzak spin for services that provide piped-in music for offices and businesses. And before long, you may hear Julio Iglesias crooning a much-softened version along with a lush symphonic accompaniment.

The third question addresses a song's versatility. Assuming a "no" to the previous question, *since this song was not originally composed in a genre which is compatible with our music mission statement, might it be reworked in a different setting or arrangement that would render it successful in a genre that IS compatible with our music mission statement?* This twofold question asks whether a song might have this kind of versatility and whether it can keep its integrity intact in an altered arrangement. Whether it's a good idea or not, most songs can be successfully rendered in a variety of other genres. However, there are standards to guide us in such a decision. Certain types of ethnic songs (such as reggae, Latin, and black gospel) are best kept in their original genres, as the musical substance of their harmony, melody, and rhythm loses its context, identity, and effectiveness when rendered outside the genre in which the songs were composed. In a well-crafted song the music serves as a metaphor—a musical image of the message it contains. A song whose integrity depends on the wedding of its message to a particular genre also should not be altered. If, for instance, hard rock has been identified as a genre for your service, it would not be advisable to convert "Silent Night" for use as a screaming hard-rocker (though it has been done, much to the chagrin of many). If the song has versatility, it earns a "yes" and passes to the next filter. "No" passes it to the fourth and final question of this filter. Again, the decision is noted on the work sheet.

Novelty songs make up a significant percentage of the worship repertoire. At St. John, the repertoire for contemporary worship is approximately 17 percent novelty songs (including some traditional Christmas and Easter hymns). Novelties are songs that don't fit or can't be fit into one of the three preferred genres identified in the music mission statement. Novelties don't define the repertoire; they vary it. This part of the filter is designed to identify which songs outside the music mission statement will work in the context of our faith community. The worship team leader asks a two-part question: *Can this song be considered for use in our congregation on the basis of its novelty appeal? And can our ensemble render the song in a high-quality performance?*

The first part of the question is designed to determine whether a song may appeal because of *how* different it is. Different must not mean *distant* from the music mission statement. Different means that despite its novelty, it connects to the context of the people who are worshiping, or who might someday be worshiping in our midst. Without such a connection, a song might fall prey to the "Laudamus Te" syndrome I described earlier, mystifying and putting worshipers at a greater distance from the message rather than drawing them nearer to it. A plainsong chant in Latin is an example of a too-distant novelty for the folks at St. John's contemporary worship service. So is rap. Using these kinds of songs would result in an "I don't get it" from nearly every worshiper in the place, initiated and uninitiated alike. "I don't get it" tells the uninitiated worshiper especially that the leaders didn't have him or her in mind when they chose this song, that "the message hasn't been translated so I can understand it," perhaps prompting the conclusion that "this [worship, church, Gospel] isn't for me."

Yet, lest we go too far in the other direction, it is essential to note that contemporary worship risks becoming so focused on the current and the vogue that we become hostages to our culture. The result is an impoverishment of our worship as we place ourselves in bondage to personal preferences. It is important to remember that the church has not taken a quantum leap from the empty tomb to the present; it has trudged onward each day for 2,000 years, and we can't be truly Christian without orienting ourselves to that journey. No organization on the planet denies its history. We build on our histories. Lathrop says, "The remembered things are not forgotten, but transformed."[5] Where we have been provides us with an environment for the encounter with God and with God's grace. We must realize that all new forms of worship spring from tradition and "be mindful of the traditions in which we are grounded."[6] Our tradition, our journey as a church serves as a center for us as we vary our worship expressions and incorporate new music. As Sally Morgenthaler states, "Contrary to popular belief, it is not culturally relevant in turn-of-the-millennium America to throw out every single piece of historic Christian communication."[7] Novelty songs, then, keep us from becoming so preference-driven that these preferences "become their own new law or usurp the place of center."[8]

Admittance to the repertoire acknowledges that a novelty song serves a purpose. Typically that purpose is to connect us to people in other times and places within a musical context that is not completely unfamiliar to most of those at worship and around us in our community. A repackaged hymn tune, such as "Beautiful Savior" (*St. Elizabeth,* or "Fairest Lord Jesus"), connects us to the church that has gone before us. A novelty song set in a reggae genre connects us to the worship of our brothers and sisters in Christ in other places. A call-and-response Psalm setting connects us to one another as we sing responsively, and connects us to the most ancient roots of our faith. A repackaged traditional hymn that is tied to a church season, such as "O Come, O Come, Emmanuel," serves to connect us to the themes of the liturgical year.

Another important quality of novelty songs is the fun factor. Novelty songs can induce a spontaneous eruption of (hold on to your seats) *fun* for the congregation in worship. "All Around Your Throne" possesses a high fun factor, with its bass line reminiscent of "La Bamba." It's not impossible to introduce clapping on the off-beat, or pattern-clapping, as indicated in Hanson and Murakani's "Clap Your Hands."

Clap Your Hands

Words and Music by Handt Hanson/Paul Murakami
© 1991 Prince of Peace Publishing/Changing Church Forum

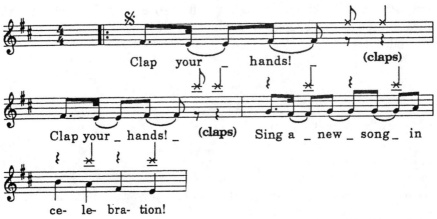

Used by permission.

The second part of the question above is practical: *Can our ensemble render the song in a quality performance?* The worship team leader is the person most capable of answering this question. He or she should understand the limitations of the musicians' abilities, and should exercise economy when considering which novelty songs might be usable. The novelty songs chosen should be those that will not tax the group's rehearsal time and can be rendered capably. The "juice ain't worth the squeeze" if it takes an inordinate amount of time to bring a novelty up to an acceptable quality. A novelty song outside the comfort zone of the band members might also be expected to induce for some a lag in confidence that can wreak havoc.

With an operational music mission statement, a repertoire of worship songs can be shaped over the long haul, with the concurrence and participation of the congregation. It serves as an objective criterion for choosing music in a realm that would otherwise be completely subjective and personal-preference-driven. It offers the congregation a way for its contemporary worship to stand the test of time, to weather the storms of changing personnel and changing leadership. It creates leadership and ministry on another level. Employing a music mission statement is an insurance policy against a new worship service "just fizzling out."

The Music Mission Statement Work Conference and "Matching Our Music To Our Mission" work sheet appear in appendixes B and C and may be photocopied. These sections are also accessible on the CD-ROM. They will help your worship team work with the process described in this text. Please refer to this chapter to make effective use of the tools in these appendixes.

CHAPTER 4

FILTER THREE:
Evaluating the Songwriting

A song might be free of heresy, and yet be boring as Kool-Aid! What we sing and say in worship must not only be accurate, it must be excellent.

—Bishop George Mocko[1]

The CD-ROM inside the cover contains musical samples of the elements of songwriting described in this chapter. Look for the ◉ symbol to indicate an audio sample on the CD-ROM. As you read, have your CD player close at hand so that you can hear the examples as they are described in the text. Each section is announced for ease of coordinating the text with the music, and the corresponding sample number will appear on your stereo's display.

The contemporary worship movement is approaching "thirty-something." More than a short-lived fad, this trend has revealed itself to be one with staying power. Since its birth in the Jesus movement, thousands and thousands of songs have been published specifically for use in contemporary worship, and with this approach to worship just revving up, we can be sure that thousands upon thousands more are yet to come. What a delightful situation! Resources for the church's worship are springing up around us like fields of daisies. Twenty years ago, we wondered where to find songs for contemporary worship. Not so these days! Newly published songs for worship virtually fall into the laps of worship planners. *Worship Leader* magazine frequently features full-page ads for new song collections, and those ads contain printed music of entire songs along with copyright permission. Yet a word of caution must be issued to churches that are picking these "daisies": Examine carefully, for among the daisies we're likely to find the more common and troublesome dandelions.

In the third filter, we consider the craft, the art, and the science of songwriting. As a team, we hold up our songs of worship and measure them against the "known factors" of what constitutes great songwriting, and judge them just as we might if we were judging a songwriting contest. This is an important, objective task for the conscientious congregation engaged in contemporary or alternative worship. In the fledgling years of the contemporary worship movement, we made an unwitting contribution to a problem in the marketplace. We demanded the new, it was supplied, and we purchased it. Yet somewhere along the way we failed to demand that our new music be great. The result is the publication of a small percentage of great material, along with a legion of material that is at best mediocre, at worst boring and simplistic, and for some, an insult to intelligence and an outright sabotage of the integrity of the worship experience.

While we go about the business of judging our own songwriting contest, we also rely in this filter on our own preferences. These preferences are a subjective companion to the objective means by which we select songs for worship. Personal preferences are an unavoidable, inescapable part of who we are as healthy people. They are God-given, as part of our createdness and human nature, and they are culture-given, as part of what we absorb from the world around us. Research in neuroscience has shown that the music of our culture has the effect of "hard-wiring" our brains, contributing to the formation of neural connections that help us make sense of our world. Jamshed Bharucha, a cognitive psychologist, explains, "When we listen to music we listen to music through cultural lenses, if you like, and the cultural lens is the way the brain is wired as a result of living in that culture."[2] He explains further, "A person in one music environment is actually likely to have a different set of brain connections—a different neural internalization of culture than somebody in another environment."[3] This hard-wiring explains why people tend to like the musical sounds of the culture in which they grew up, why the sounds of a musical scale in Dublin may sound distasteful and dissonant to a listener in Zimbabwe or Brazil.[4]

Contemporary worship has been criticized by traditionalists for "pandering to personal preferences," but this new research shows us that preferences are not merely subjective likes and dislikes that change on the wind of current trends; they are part of the amazing work of the brain in collating information from the world around us, providing a basis for how we think and function. The music we like doesn't just "please" us; it shapes us and helps our minds to understand and operate in a world that is downloading limitless quantities of data into our brains. If we provide the kind of music people prefer, there are neurological explanations for why we are making worship more understandable and more hospitable to them.

As partners in the process of song evaluation, we may rely on our preferences to help guide us in song selection. The "subjective" element of acknowledging personal preference in this filter gives us the ability to say, "Even though that's technically an awkward leap in the voice line, I really like it. It works for me." It gives us the ability to override a songwriting "minus" with a human element, a personal preference "plus."

Personal tastes should not, however, be used alone in song evaluation without the more objective elements of the evaluative process. Nor should preference be allowed to become the exclusive subjective measuring stick of one person. The opinions of the entire team are needed in this process. When the team is involved, the repertoire has the "stamp" of many participants, and the subjective and objective evaluations are based on the contributions of many rather than one. The congregation should not rely on one person's vision, songwriting knowledge, or preferences to ensure continuing evolution of the repertoire.

There are important reasons for exercising this filter of musicality and songwriting basics in a team process. First, bringing the team into the process equips team members to be leaders and stakeholders in the integrity of worship. It demystifies the process of song selection. It creates confidence in the songs chosen. Bringing in the team provides a twofold accountability—accountability of the leader to the team as he or she guides the development of a repertoire, and of the team to the congregation as it presents great songs to enhance the worship of the community of faith. It eliminates the top-down approach so common in typical committee processes. It assures the continuity of choosing great songs as the repertoire evolves over time, and helps create agreement about which songs have longevity and which ones will most likely serve their purpose and then be retired. It also assures the continuity of a repertoire that is not joined at the hip to a particular worship leader. The personnel can change without the repertoire's suffering the loss of that person's "stamp." The congregation never has to wonder, "What would we do without our worship team leader? Would this all blow away without her?"

Songwriting Evaluation: The Objective Criteria

Two separate, distinct factors constitute a great song. Music and lyrics are the central elements of songwriting. Evaluation of songwriting starts with these two elements and probes the breadth and depth of the qualities in each. For the musical element of songwriting, evaluation is based on these essential features: form, melody, harmony, and rhythm. For the lyric element of songwriting, evaluation is based on lyric quality and construction, considering also innovation, clarity, imagery, climax, rhyme, economy of wording, and appeal. For the church's worship, it is also important to evaluate the lyric's use of colloquialism and vernacular, as well as anachronism and archaic language. The vantage point of the lyric also needs to be observed. From whose perspective is the song sung? This aspect helps the team understand how the song might be used in worship (see chapter 5, "Filter Four, Plugging Our Music into Our Worship").

Musical Factors of Songwriting

The rest of this chapter is written with the assumption that the reader is a musician. If you're not a musician, you may want to have one handy if you're confused about the terminology or musical concepts presented. None of the material is too difficult or technical, but a friendly musician might be helpful for maximum understanding of the elements of a good song.

Identifiable Form

A good song for worship should have an identifiable form. The simplest form is the "through-composed" song. "Through-composed" doesn't mean patternless; it does mean that the patterns are small and subtle. In these songs, there is little repetition of melodic motives, and when there is repetition, it generally involves only a small part of the melody, which is likely to head in a different direction each time it's used in the song. Songs in this form are typically quite short, have simple lyrics, and are sung repeatedly. "He Is Exalted," by Twila Paris, is a popular through-composed song. Listen to example 1 on the CD. The "chorus" is a variation ◎

of the through-composed song form. Originally, the chorus was exactly that—a chorus separated from a longer, more complex song and isolated for use in worship. Many congregations use the choruses of the popular worship songs "Awesome God," by Rich Mullins, or "Step By Step," by Mullins and Beaker, in this way; few of those who sing these staples of the repertoire are even aware that these songs have verses. Often a through-composed song is called a chorus because the properties are so similar.

The "verse-chorus" song form is the most common one for worship. It has an identifiable chorus, expressing the main message of the song, and one or more verses, which lead each time to the chorus. The verses contain the development, application, or elaboration of the ideas presented in the chorus. Graham Kendrick's "Shine, Jesus, Shine" is written in verse-chorus form. Listen to example 2 on the CD. ◎

The "AB" form (and all of its permutations; i.e., ABABA, AABBA, etc.) is also common in the contemporary worship repertoire. In the AB forms, neither the A nor the B section seems to be an identifiable chorus or verse. Each is equally strong, and supports the other; yet they are distinctively different. The AB form does not typically have multiple verses for this reason. "Give Thanks," by Henry Smith, is an example of a song in AB form, and can be heard in example 3 of the CD. ◎

A similar form is the ABC form, heard here in example 4, "My God ◎ Reigns," by Darrell Evans. Like "Give Thanks," it has no identifiable chorus. Each section is distinctly different and stands alone musically. The lyrics tie it all together.

The "verse-chorus-bridge" song form is similar to the verse-chorus form, except that it adds new musical and lyric material (not previously introduced in the verse or chorus), which is most often placed just before the last chorus. The bridge lyrics and musical elements further deepen the meaning of the chorus. The bridge sometimes takes the song into a new key. "Glorious God," by David Baroni, Bob Fitts, Paul Smith, and Claire Cloninger, is a congregational song that incorporates this form. Hear it in example 5. ◎

A newer verse-chorus song form, popularized in the songwriting of the 1990s, includes a "ramp" or "channel" as the last part of the verse, serving specifically to create a more exciting connection of the verse to the chorus. The ramp of the verse musically boosts the approach into the chorus. Consider the now-famous "God is great, God is good" ramp from Joan Osborne's 1996 secular hit, "What if God Was One of Us." Listen to the

ramp in my "All Things Work for Good" in example 6. Ramps are, at this
writing, more likely to be found in the hit songs of contemporary Christian
music and the secular mainstream than in the worship repertoire, yet it is
likely that the contemporary writers of worship songs will increasingly
bring this fresh trend to the crafting of new songs for worship.

An identifiable form gives a song a structure and context that make it
understandable. In the activity of listening to or singing a new song, the
human mind works to connect that new song to something it already knows.
When the melody, words, or other elements of a song are unfamiliar, then
at the very least the form must be familiar. As Westerners surrounded by
Western music, we have a deeply entrenched musical code which we may
not know we subscribe to, but which we nonetheless expect to be followed.
That code includes some manipulation of repeated musical patterns, and
the specific structure of repetition gives a song one of the identifiable forms
described above. In worship as in culture, we need to acknowledge that an
identifiable form gives us quick access and a kind of "road map" to a song;
it provides the first and most important open door when everything else
about the song is unknown. When a song's form does not match one of these
identifiable forms or a variation thereof, we can confidently reject it as
inadequate for use in worship.

Singable Melody

The melody is the backbone of the song. If the melody is excellent and
singable, it has the potential to carry an otherwise average song into the
category of greatness. All other elements of the song must connect
meaningfully and successfully to the melody. In worship, a melody can't
simply be beautiful for its own sake, as a melody in a Beethoven piano
sonata might be. It has to be beautiful in terms of its usefulness for singing
by a group of nonmusicians who have never rehearsed it or even heard it
before being invited to jump in and sing it.

One essential element of a good melody for a worship song is that its
phrase lengths are short enough to be memorable and long enough to be
interesting. Melodic phrases that are too short are boring and
unimaginative, and sound overrepetitive (example 7); phrases that are too
long tend to silence the singers because they are perceived as difficult and
do not afford an obvious opportunity to take a breath (example 8). Pattern

and the creative use of repetition are important in a good melody. Kurt Kaiser's "Oh How He Loves You and Me," a through-composed song, is an excellent example of pattern and creative use of repetition in the melody. It incorporates a stepwise melody, which is then simply sequenced up (example 9). The melody is established starting on the *mi* step of the scale, and is then repeated starting on *la* of the scale. It is then turned in a new stepwise direction, using repeated simple downward sequencing, ending with an effective and simple melodic repetition. A great melody has an identifiable melodic climax. Listen again to "Oh How He Loves You and Me." Do you hear the melodic climax? It's quite obvious even to the nonmusician. The idea of melodic climax is "in the ears" of anyone who listens to contemporary music. A good melodic climax makes good musical sense; it draws attention to itself and creates a sense of musical importance in one part of the melody.

To be useful for group singing, a great worship song must also possess melodic qualities that make it hospitable—that is, singable in the range comfortable for most people. A simple guideline for acceptable range is one octave, more or less. A few steps more than an octave will create no problem in most songs, but a melody should be carefully evaluated if its range exceeds an octave plus a fifth, since this expansive range might indicate that the song contains awkward leaps, which can make the song quite difficult to sing (example 10). Similarly, a range of less than one octave could indicate the overuse of a small group of notes, resulting in a boring melody (example 11). The "comfort zone" for a voice or group of voices singing contemporary music is a bit lower than for standard hymnody. Since print music for congregational singing is scored in treble clef, a congregation gathered for contemporary or alternative worship possesses a range generally from A below middle C to D an octave and a half above. Songs with notes outside this range could generally be perceived by the congregation as "too low" and "too high," respectively. A low or high tessitura—that is, the clustering of melodic material at either the low end or the high end of the range—is also likely to produce similar criticism (examples 12 and 13). Considering range is important because staying within the comfortable range of a song helps make the melody accessible for the congregation. It is extending musical "common courtesy" to those invited to sing. Moving the key of the song up or down (transposing) is a quick and easy fix for a song keyed too low or too high in its printed or recorded form. The lead sheet format most ensemble musicians use lends itself to easy transposition using the circle of fifths (see *The New Harvard Dictionary of Music* for more information on transposing and the circle of fifths).

Another quality of the hospitable melody is a fairly predictable, stepwise voice leading with no awkward leaps. Interval leaps of more than a third or fourth should be evaluated for difficulty. With a leap larger than a fourth, check to see if the leap leads to some stepwise motive. Also, check the harmony in the accompaniment or guitar chords to see if the leaps correspond to the underlying harmony. If the leaps outline the chords of the harmony, chances are that they will be followed by the congregation without too much trouble, as in Hanson's "Make My Life a Candle" (example 14).

Interesting Harmony

The harmonic structure that underlies a melody gives it character. Harmony, more than any other musical aspect of contemporary music, evokes feelings and images, and pairs those feelings and images with the melody. The chords that make up the accompaniment (however they are styled rhythmically) can render a song "peaceful," "restless," "dramatic," or "energetic." They can even indicate "somber" versus "celebrative." On the CD, listen to the two variations of Laurie Klein's "I Love You, Lord," example 15. In these samples, the melody is the same while the underlying harmonic treatment varies. The first example is the standard harmonization, and the second uses harmonic variations, creating an entirely different feeling for the melody.

Contemporary worship has put the church's song into new harmonic territory. While traditional hymns typically shift harmonically with every beat, songs for contemporary and alternative worship do not. More typically, they will shift every measure or half-measure. Listen to "Prayer of St. Francis," by Carey Creed, example 16. This choice results in a single chord supporting more of the melody than in standard hymnody. The harmonic movement in contemporary worship songs can therefore sound overly simple and uninteresting. Harmony in worship songs should be evaluated for complexity and harmonic interest. Songs that are harmonically simple (using only chords I, IV and V, for instance) can end up sounding like Sunday school or camp songs. The songs of worship need to have a "beefier" harmonic structure than the songs we've sung as children or around the campfire. If only three chords are indicated in the guitar chart of a song, listen and evaluate carefully.

Similarly, the harmonic structure of a song ought to have an element of predictability. Western music mandates certain resolutions of certain chords; musicians generally agree that the only logical resolutions of an Asus4 chord are to A major (example 17) or to E major, which recalls the familiar hymn-closing "A-men." Other alternatives sound absurd, and quite "wrong" to our ears. With most other harmonic progressions, alternatives are available. A good harmonic progression goes most often with the "defaults" but also takes a few risks and offers some harmonic surprises. Listen to example 18, "From the Ashes," which incorporates some jazzlike harmonic progressions. Though this tune takes us down an eyebrow-raising harmonic road, it works! The surprise we hear serves also to delight us, and when we participate in singing the song, we subconsciously congratulate ourselves for "getting it" even though it's a bit outside the lines of its soft-pop styling. This harmony challenges us and helps us succeed. We must be careful when taking harmonic risks that they actually "work" for the ears of those assembled in worship. Sometimes they don't. Worship is not the place to take musical risks that push the musical sensibilities of the singers. This caution goes for melody, harmony, and rhythm.

The marriage of melody and harmony is also important. Melody and harmony must work together as a cogent unit. When one fights the other, this inhospitable union results in a less-than-singable result. Listen to example 19. A repeated melodic pattern operates above an interesting harmony. Independent of one another they work fine, but together they "clash" in the second phrase. In an effort to keep the pattern moving, the melody is force-fit. In song selection, it is necessary to identify and discard songs that have a less-than-successful marriage of melody and harmony. The inevitable result of using a song with a poor match of melody and harmony is the silencing of the singers. Even when the fault lies with the song and its harmony, the singer assumes that he or she isn't singing the song correctly or can't sing it correctly, so the "I don't get it; therefore I'll close my mouth" syndrome takes over.

Modulating the key in the course of a song is a powerful metaphor-bearer. This technique of harmonic manipulation is being used increasingly in contemporary worship music to bring a heightened emotional element to a song. The simple verse-chorus "There's a Song," by Handt Hanson (example 20) has two key changes written into the accompaniment. Changing keys creates musical excitement; it provides an "exclamation point." In a simple song, such as the five-verse "There's A Song," it also helps to keep things interesting. However, as in grammar, when this exclamation point is overused in worship, one begins to wonder, "Is all this really as exciting as they're trying to tell me it is?" Key changes should therefore be used sparingly. Overused, they become suspect and lose their potency as metaphor-bearers.

Rhythm

Often, we think of rhythm as simply "the beat." Much more than just the beat that our toes are tapping, rhythm applies to all aspects of a song, including the melody and the harmony. The differences between standard hymns and contemporary songs in their melodic and harmonic elements are minute in comparison to the profound differences in rhythm. Traditional hymnody befriended the quarter note and the half note; contemporary worship music has befriended a rhythmic complexity far exceeding that of standard hymnody. Most notably, syncopation is the element that characterizes the rhythmic landscape of contemporary worship music. Syncopation is in the ear of the people; its fingerprints are all over the music of popular culture. In fact, songs that are mostly quarter notes and relatively free of syncopation are seen as so unengaging that they are almost entirely disregarded in this repertoire. Even in the most contemplative songs of the contemporary worship repertoire, there can be rich rhythmic complexity and syncopation, as in Paul Baloche's "Heal Me, Oh Lord" (example 21).

Yet syncopation must be used in careful proportion to be understood and followed in group singing. Syncopated rhythms strung together with accents on successive off-beats can cause problems for group singing. Listen to example 22, where I have demonstrated the effect of "trailed syncopation." When syncopation is strung across the downbeat over several measures, the likelihood that people will get lost increases. Syncopation in the song of the people should be hospitable and fairly predictable.

Rhythm should have a careful and well-crafted connection to the melody and the harmony. (The function of lyrics in this partnership is also extremely important, and will be considered in detail in the section below.) Consider how Rodgers and Hammerstein's "Oh, What A Beautiful Mornin'" might come across with just a slight alteration in the rhythm of this famous melody. Sing the song to yourself, and make the note falling on the first syllable of "mornin'" short instead of long. Doing so significantly disturbs its effect in the context of the melody. A rhythmic sensitivity to the leading of the melody and harmony is one ingredient of great songwriting.

One cannot consider rhythm without also considering tempo. Whether a song is intended to be fast or slow, success can depend in large part upon small variations in tempo. Frequently, up-tempo songs for contemporary worship can seem "too fast" and have the effect of silencing the congregation. Tempos should be comfortable for the congregation. As the congregation learns a song, the beat can be "picked up" to provide greater interest and challenge, and to render the song in a style closer to the composer's intentions.

Accompaniments

The music of contemporary and alternative worship comes with a large proviso: "Do your own thing" seems to apply to just about everything in print. Very little is published with sophisticated (or even adequate) accompaniments that can be played as written. Most printed music is either just a voice line or a simple hymnlike arrangement of one or more voice lines plus guitar chords; these should not be interpreted as fully arranged keyboard accompaniments. The publishers assume that the ensemble players will be able to derive their parts from this basic "lead sheet" or song-sheet format, and that they will imbue the song with life and character in their playing and artistry. The print music merely serves as an aid to show "how the song goes." There are exceptions, as in the lovely keyboard accompaniments published by the Minneapolis-based Changing Church. The praise-and-worship giant Integrity is now offering more sophisticated arrangements as well. Most accompaniments, however, are skeletal blueprints that need a large dose of artistry added to enliven them.

Lyric Factors in Songwriting

Lyrics are the heart and soul of a song for worship. The lyrics are the most obvious metaphor-bearers of our faith. As previously described in the "Assessing Theology" filter, it is essential that the lyrics be truthful. This section will explore the requirement that lyrics also be artful in content and construction.

High-Quality Content

The texts of our songs of faith have, over the centuries, featured a variety of word-use genres. Direct Scripture quotations were featured in plainsong chant and the great masses and motets, and beautiful poetry was featured in the hymns of John and Charles Wesley. Our songs of faith have evoked powerful images, have given inspiration and comfort, and have praised and petitioned the Maker. Today, more than ever, songs for worship are being asked to approach the faith in new ways. Acknowledging the "front door" approach of the songs of the past, contemporary songs for worship increasingly come through a side door or even a back door to be useful to the people for whom the front door may be a closed door.

Innovation is the watchword for lyrics in contemporary worship music. The language we use to speak our doctrine and beliefs is increasingly less "churchy," free from words and images that form the language of the initiated, who have experience with the verbal coinage of traditional worship.

Consider William Cowper's eighteenth-century hymn text "There Is a Fountain Filled with Blood." The first line creates such a powerful visual image that for the uninitiated, the picture is like something out of a Stephen King novel—frightening, gory, and horrifying. The image is so evocative that the message of the text may be lost as the seeker ponders that awful picture. True, its power for the believer is one of deep comfort and the means of our salvation, but for the nonbeliever, it pulls up the drawbridge. The message of our redemption through Christ's work on the cross comes through an innovative use of words in Handt Hanson's "Leave Your Heart with Me."

You can lay your heavy heart at my feet and make a new start.
You can drop your weight of sin on my cross and start again.
You can leave your worries far behind: you can give your guilt to
   me.
For lonely as it seems you can leave your heart with me.

The need for lyric innovation calls on the writers of contemporary worship music to express the ideas and doctrines at the heart of our faith with new images that spring from the context and resources of popular culture. Employing the innovation available in local and contemporary metaphors makes good sense in the effort to make the Christian message relevant to just about anyone who comes through the door.

Clarity of message is important in lyrics for contemporary worship music. A lyric should "get to the point" quickly, and one should be able to grasp the essential idea without too much digging. A clear message lets singers know what's important and exactly what's being sung about. It sends up a thematic flare as the lyrics are woven together effectively to create a distinct idea or image. Imagine "More Precious Than Silver" if it were written this way:

Lord, You are more precious than silver.
Lord, You save me from my troubles.
Lord, You are a friend to the poor.
Nothing on this earth is like You.

What's the song about? Well, it's about God. It proclaims some truths about God. But see how lyricist Lynn DeShazo really put this lyric together:

Lord, You are more precious than silver.
Lord, You are more costly than gold.
Lord, You are more beautiful than diamonds,
And nothing I desire compares with You.

This lyric has clarity. It is about how much I value God, giving the specific details of how much I value God. Great songs for worship ought to possess this kind of clarity. Another point worth considering is the popularity and influence of the New Age movement, which advocates a "wide way" in faith and belief. Our songs for worship ought to be convincingly Christian, should not create confusion with any other god, and should dare to name our God in any of God's triune manifestations. References to God that are only "He" or "You" are not clear enough today and are therefore subject to criticism. Although a good many songs in the repertoire do not effectively name God, using such songs in worship should be done in concert with a selection of songs that *do* name God. Consider these verses I wrote for "Into the Life":

> Spirit, God, Abba, be with us now,
> We are just travellers in the night on the way.
> Jesus, Lord, our brother, be with us now,
> We are Your people, You're the light day to day.
>
> Prince of Peace, Savior, be with us now,
> Teach us to love and be our song on the way.
> Helper, friend, Maker, be with us now,
> Deep in our hearts You keep us strong day to day.

Similarly, great lyrics for worship possess economy of expression. It doesn't take a whole mittful of words to get the point across. Each word contributes meaningfully to the idea or image of the lyric, with no words to spare. The song should be so tight lyrically that the removal of any word reduces its meaning. An excess of words is a danger sign that a song may be too broad in scope. Frequent repetition of words is a danger sign for a boring, too-simple lyric.

Great songs for worship contain lively images. The most powerful songs evoke visual, aural, and emotional images, touching the singer at different levels. The song takes form in the mind's eye complete with picture, sound, and emotion. Consider the lyrics of "Cares Chorus," by Kelly Willard:

I cast all my cares upon You.
I lay all of my burdens down at Your feet.
And anytime that I don't know what to do,
I will cast all my cares upon You.

This song creates visual, aural, and emotional images, and in so doing creates a powerful metaphor for comfort and forgiveness. It also takes an innovative approach to carrying a biblical text. It is important that the images created are familiar ones, images that resonate with current cultural trends and the experience of the people. For instance, a contemporary song that sets up images of war, fighting, and soldiering is no longer politically correct, even though it has biblical and confessional bases in many denominations, and even though many people know and have experienced the horrors of war. Our pastoral prayers are continually invoking peace, and we err when we proceed to sing a song that glorifies war. Only within an appropriate context, paired with a sermon about the forces of darkness warring upon the righteous, may such a song be useful.

Climax is another element of a great lyric. It is the point toward which all the other words aim; and it is the point from which all the other words flow. Climax in the lyric has an element of surprise. Generally not a repeated phrase or a lyric "hook," the climax is the "a-ha" of a lyric. The climax tells you something important that the rest of the lyric did not. Hanson's "We Love You" has an effective climax in the chorus:

We are here to say we love you.
We are here to say we know your love is true.
We can say these words because you said them first.
You said them on the cross, your blood became the cost for love.

The climax in line four provides a big payoff and delivers a punch. It contains an ultimate truth, and the song would be less forceful without it. A lyric climax is spiritually satisfying, and without a lyric climax, we as worshipers are left still searching for the hope that we invested in the song when we began singing it.

Rhyme, for the most part, is becoming less important as an element of lyric writing. Lyrics have taken a radical departure, and few of the newest songs for worship follow the strict metrical and rhyme schemes of the poetry that served as hymn texts in the past. End-of-phrase rhyming is being replaced by a more complex intraphrase or internal rhyming, as in these two phrases from the song above, "You can lay your heavy *heart* at my feet / and make a new *start.*" The end-of-phrase words are *feet* and *start*, but Hanson rhymes a word from the middle of the first phrase, *heart,* with the last word of the second phrase, *start,* creating an internal rhyme. The necessity for rhyme is diminishing overall, yet where rhyme is present it must be innovative. There have been enough songs that rhyme *dove* and *love, Lord* and *adored.* These rhyming pairs are so overused that we ought to respond, "Oh no, not again," when we see them coming.

Yet, lest we take too many liberties with our poetry, the rhymes must still create cogent images that resonate with common word usage. Making good sense always takes priority over perfect rhyme. When a rhyme is achieved at the expense of making good sense, the lyric has failed, and sounds naïve to the singer. Take this example: "Son of God, of human birth, came to heal this sinful earth . . ." The rhyme works, but the image misses the mark, as the earth is not sinful—the people upon it are. While we can appreciate the writer's innovation, the fact remains that the earth cannot generate sin, and it was for the healing of the soul that Christ came.

Use of colloquialisms in lyrics should be exercised with caution, especially since they can be misinterpreted, misunderstood, or not understood at all by those outside an in-group circle of usage. An example is found in the Lester Lewis song "Winna, Mon." Out of context, the title seems to have no meaning; it is only in hearing or singing this fun, Jamaican-sounding, island-beat tune that we "get it," as the lyric describes Satan as the loser and Jesus as the victor, the *winna, mon.*

Colloquialisms are faddish and cliquish. We should question whether they have any place in the lyrics of our congregational songs of faith, since they may preclude some people from understanding the message. At the same time, this song may be extremely successful as a special music offering, performed by the band and singers in an anthem slot. The surprise of understanding the title in the midst of hearing the song might work well to enhance the listener's enjoyment of the service.

It may be important to consider how the church's historic language, its doctrine, and its theologies might now be seen by the unchurched visitor as "colloquial," and to use its words with caution. Many unchurched people will have no clue as to what *justification, redemption,* or *salvific* might mean.

However, use of vernacular is a friend to the writer of contemporary worship songs, just as it was to Martin Luther when he began translating the mass into German. How effective would a missionary be in a Spanish-speaking country if she went there speaking only English? Likewise, our lyrics need to speak the language of those who will gather with us in worship. To be most effective, lyrics should not only be in the same language, but should mirror the idioms and mannerisms by which the people in the local culture express themselves. Beyond mere words, vernacular encompasses grammar and sentence structure. Lyrics should avoid unusual word placement that would not occur in normal speech. For example, consider this line from a hymn: "The royal banners forward go. . ." No one from any age or cultural group that I've ever met would elect to express the idea in this way, except perhaps a person translating another language into English. Why should we ask people to sing in sentence structures unlike any they would use in normal speech? Our contemporary songs for worship should represent the language of the people, with their way of expressing ideas. They should be able to acknowledge that "this song can be my song."

Believers in other times used words appropriate to their own era in worship. To the extent that we desire to be connected to the church of God in every age, older songs that include archaic language have value because they give us that connection.

However, as strange as it may seem, use of anachronism and archaic language persists in the contemporary repertoire, despite the commonsense approach that songs in a contemporary style should use contemporary language. Anachronism in lyrics can be defined as the use of any figure of speech or words which, by their very usage, indicate attachment to values and realities of another time, and not this current one. "Exclusive" language in lyrics can rightly be criticized as anachronism. Similarly, archaic language has no place in the lyrics of the contemporary worship repertoire. No one today speaks in King James English, and it should not be imported into our contemporary songs from its place in history. "Thy," as a word, is no holier than "Your." Archaic words from any source should be avoided by the writers of lyrics for the faith songs of today.

High-Quality Lyric Construction

Evaluation of lyric construction requires seeing the lyric in its relationship to other elements of the song. A well-constructed lyric is excellently married to the melody and the rhythm. Principally, the accented syllables of words must match both the accented beats of the song and the accented notes of the melody to work well together. Consider the word "celebrate." Its accented syllable is the first one. If one spoke this word with an accent on the second or third syllable, it would sound strange. The use of the word "celebrate" in a song lyric should not require that any syllable other than the dominant one be emphasized by accents occurring in the melody or rhythm. Yet songwriters frequently pair nondominant syllables in lyrics with dominant accents in the melody and/or rhythm (listen to example 23). ◎ This is a sign of less-than-careful songwriting, and again requires us to sing in a manner in which we would never speak. Such lyrics create a no-win situation: Not only are we using words that we would never speak in exactly this way; we are asking a song to do something it cannot do. A song cannot be an accurate or adequate metaphor-bearer of the faith if it has not been carefully and skillfully crafted for this important task.

Another common fault in lyric construction of worship songs is a mismatch of lyric ideas and musical ideas. The lyric idea should fit "like a glove" with the song's musical ideas. In a well-crafted song, the wedding of lyric to music is so effective that they enhance each other. A song about joy, for example, would be completely at home in a bouncy, major-key melody. Cast in a slow, haunting, or plodding minor-key tune, a lyric focused on joy fails to "resonate" effectively with its music. The lyrics fight the melody, and the melody pulls the rug out from under the lyrics. Or consider a praise song with the lyrics, "We lift our voices high . . ." and imagine singing them in a descending stepwise melody. When the lyrics don't mirror the musical images, a song is rendered less effective. This is a perfect lyric for an ascending melody line: Each element of the phrase echoes the other, and they make perfect sense together (example 24). The ◎ classical composers used this kind of lyric "painting" liberally. Handel's *Messiah* is full of such devices; consider the bass recitative in which the soloist sings, ". . . and I will shake . . ." The long, fast melismatic passage that carries the word "shake" quite literally shakes.

Lyric Orientation

An important aspect of a lyric is its basic vantage point. As we sing this song, whom does the song claim to represent, me or us? Is it sung from the perspective of someone other than me or us? Does this song speak as a prophetic voice, or even God's voice? Is this song *about* God; a song that proclaims? Or is it addressed *to* God—a prayer or song of praise? Is it about something we do or something that happens in the midst of worship? A song with a "we/us" orientation has a horizontal quality. It highlights the connection of all gathered for worship and the importance of community in our worship expression. It connects us to our neighbors in worship and makes the song a public event. A song with an "I/me" orientation has a vertical quality. It highlights the connection between the individual and God in worship and makes the song a private event. The majority of the contemporary worship repertoire features the song of the individual, and for this reason, the contemporary worship movement has been criticized for helping to promote the rampant individualism that plagues our culture. It is important that songs of faith not be sung from the exclusive orientation of the individual to God, turning worship into a "Jesus and me" event. The next filter on song use will pursue this matter more thoroughly.

How to Use the 'Evaluating the Songwriting' Filter

The best way to use the "Evaluating the Songwriting" filter is to invite the team to participate in three half-day work conferences per year to focus exclusively on this filter. Before these work conferences, a group of songs is selected by the worship team leader to be presented to the team. These songs have already passed the "Assessing Theology" and "Matching our Music to Our Mission" filters, and can be presented with a degree of confidence for the consideration of the entire team. As the song is played and sung through by the worship team leader or other musician, each team member will complete an "Evaluating the Songwriting" work sheet on the song presented (see appendix D). Group discussion follows each presentation, allowing team members to voice their observations and feelings about the songs. The scoring sheets are then reviewed and averaged, and overall scores are assigned to each song. Songs with fewer than ten points receive a failing score, and songs with fewer than 15 need to be carefully evaluated for appropriateness in your context. Songs with more than 15 points receive a passing evaluation.

Final discussion is held after the scores are tabulated to inform the team which songs passed this filter and which will accordingly be used in worship, to satisfy the team that these outcomes are an accurate reflection of its work, to establish concurrence on the outcomes, and to allow the group to set aside a song for further discussion and evaluation if there is strong disagreement about a song's "passing" or "failing" status. Such a song should be set aside until the next "Evaluating the Songwriting" work conference. Passing songs move on to the fourth filter for determination of how and when the song might be used in worship.

The work of evaluating songs for worship as I've described it in these three filters may seem nit-picking to some. It does, however, give us sure footing for creating a repertoire of the very best songs we can offer to God at each worship service. When we hold our songs of worship up to the light, we can be assured that when we use them in worship, they will serve as potent musical experiences in which we can encounter God, the risen Christ, and the Holy Spirit.

CHAPTER 5

FILTER FOUR:
Plugging Our Music
into Our Worship

In a situation in which music is at odds with what is supposed to be happening, my whole sense of order . . . is thrown out of kilter.

—Robert Webber[1]

Laws written to determine appropriate uses for land contain a phrase helpful for our fourth filter. "Highest and best use" describes the most fitting and beneficial use of a plot or tract of land, the ways in which it can most successfully serve the ultimate needs of its owners, purchasers, or users. "Highest and best use" theory presupposes that land is better for certain purposes than others. For instance, land that is mostly clay-based and rocky will not have its highest and best use in farming. It might be excellent for housing or business. When part of my front yard is bought by the state to become a right-of-way for the eventual widening of the road, the state successfully claims that the highest and best use of that part of my yard is for the increased flow of traffic in the community. Despite my protests, "highest and best use" theory wins the day (and my flowering dogwood).

In determining how we use songs in contemporary and alternative worship, "highest and best use" theory comes into play in significant ways. Many elements of a song determine whether it is useful for certain functions and less useful for others. Lyrics, subject matter, musical style, and even tempo can give us clues as to how to include a song in worship for its highest and best use. This filter champions the notion that we should use songs only in the capacity of their highest and best use. Used outside of that realm, the songs won't serve our worship as effectively as they could, they won't be successful in doing what we ask them to do, and they may confuse or distract worshipers and interrupt the flow of worship rather than enhance it.

Another analogy: Many old-growth hardwood forests of the South have been prized for the wonderful wood they provide for the making of fine furniture. Yet more and more often, these forests are being harvested for chip factories, which turn wood to pulp for fiberboard or paper products. The tree farmers and landowners of today are impatient, and want to reap the profits of their crop sooner rather than later, despite the fact that later the trees would be worth much more money as veneers for fine furniture. Harvested early, the beautiful hardwoods with the potential to become costly pieces of furniture are no more valuable than scrub pine and other soft, fast-growing trees. As worship team leaders and curators of our worship repertoire, we must be like patient tree farmers, taking the time and care to make our songs work for our congregations in the best and most spiritually valuable way. This way, we load our one-hour services with music that makes the experience of worship rich and powerful from beginning to end, and the songs function like a majestic old oak destined to become a dining-room table instead of a cardboard box.

This filter assumes that no matter what form of worship a church has embraced, worship that includes the Lord's Supper has something of a fourfold pattern. (Worship without the meal has something of a threefold pattern). Gathering, hearing, and responding to the Word; participating in the meal; and sending are the basic actions of those gathered for worship. This shape can be modified for a service that does not include the meal and that might include other events (such as baptism, reception of new members, and other special elements). For simplicity's sake, I will describe the workings of this filter within the fourfold pattern described above.

Some congregations might object to the idea that their worship has any predisposed pattern at all. Yet the fourfold pattern need not have ritual written all over it. Even a praise-and-prayer service has a pattern—most likely, threefold. A service described only as "loose, comfortable, and casual" also has something of a pattern, even if the people aren't reading from worship folders or hymnbooks. We acknowledge the basic need for some particular *way* to begin worship. We start with something welcoming, an act that helps set the tone and helps make worshipers comfortable. We move into some way that the Gospel is shared. We embellish the Gospel with a lively word, a way of describing it, making it important and useful to us today. Sharing the Lord's Supper is not just the handing out of a small snack. It comes with words and actions of explaining, recounting, and inviting. Similarly, sending helps us know the service is ending, helps us get up and go, and can help us remember what we came for and what we learned along the way. *The songs of worship can effectively support and enhance these worship elements, as each one bears some metaphorical aspect of the qualities and functions of gathering, word, meal, or sending.* All that is required is careful examination to determine which songs are best at supporting which functions.

Certain songs are particularly useful for certain elements of worship. A praise song generally can't do the job of a sending song, and a song sung from the perspective of the individual can't do the job of a gathering song. What we need is a commonsense approach to using songs in way that helps make the worship experience seamless and flowing. Such an approach requires that the choice of music serve the ultimate goal of successfully engaging the community in worship.

Sally Morgenthaler suggests an hourglass shape for song use (see fig. 4). The top of the hourglass represents gathering. It is the least intimate, most high-energy, most public and most community-oriented expression. The middle of the hourglass is the most intimate, lowest-energy, highest in emotional intensity, most private and individual-oriented expression, generally (and not surprisingly) found in the middle of the service. Toward the end of the service, music takes the community back into a less intimate, high-energy, community expression in the sending.

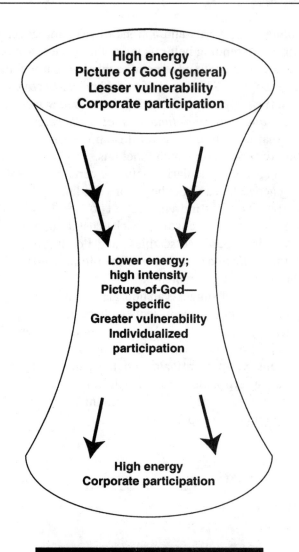

Figure 4

"The Worship Hourglass," taken from *Worship Evangelism*, by Sally Morgenthaler.
Copyright © 1995 by Sally Morgenthaler.
Used by permission of Zondervan Publishing House.

Speaker, author, and teacher Robert Webber elaborates on Morgenthaler's model by further defining use of music for worship.[2] See appendix E for a chart that sets out these principles for song use and worship planning. Webber believes that the initial action of gathering for worship should clearly be an invitation, should be the unmistakable voice of all of us (as opposed to just "me"), and should include a description of what we're doing here. It is not just an upbeat praise song. Consider the chorus of "Come to the River of Life," by Don Moen and Claire Cloninger:

> Come to the river of life, you will find healing here;
> Come to the river of life, come and drink freely here.
> Come if your heart is searching, come if your soul is thirsty;
> Draw near and drink of the mercy of Jesus Christ at the river of life.

Only one such song is needed to establish these key principles of gathering: all are invited to come, we are here to worship God, and we all participate in the actions of worship. Following the initial gathering song, Webber suggests moving into a song or section of songs that describe God. These are songs that proclaim, songs that tell about God and what God has done and continues to do among God's people. Ideally, the songs in this section continue to represent the voice of the community. These songs proclaiming God have overtones of praise, but in the purest sense, they are not praise songs. Consider the lyrics of the first verse of "Great is the Lord," by Michael W. Smith and Deborah D. Smith:

> Great is the Lord, He is holy and just,
> By His power we trust in His love.
> Great is the Lord, He is faithful and true,
> By His mercy He proves He is love.
> Great is the Lord and worthy of glory,
> Great is the Lord and worthy of praise.
> Great is the Lord, now lift up your voice, now lift up your voice:
> Great is the Lord! Great is the Lord!

It surely feels like praise, but it is proclamation. And as such, it beautifully sets up the next song or section of songs—the praise songs. This sequence works so well because the songs of proclamation remind worshipers and allow them to realize why we ought to praise God. Moving from this point into songs directed *to* God makes perfect sense. Now is the time for the praise song. The people gathered have acknowledged why they've gathered, they've sung about God's greatness, and now they address God directly in songs to glorify, thank, and honor God. Praise songs are purely praise; they are not petition or proclamation. "We Bow Down," by Twila Paris, is such a song:

You are Lord of creation and Lord of my life,
Lord of the land and the sea;
You were Lord of the heavens before there was time,
And Lord of all lords You will be.
We bow down and we worship You, Lord.
We bow down and we worship You, Lord.
We bow down and we worship You, Lord,
Lord of all lords You will be.

The end of the praise section is the perfect place for a song or songs sung from the perspective of the individual. Following Morgenthaler's model, this shift takes the flow of worship smoothly from the most public toward the more private expression. Singing from the perspective of "me" is more private than singing from that of "us," even amid the community. Praise songs are the songs of love, sung from the lover to the beloved; in worship, the beloved is God. The I-perspective praise song is also a good place to look for a higher emotional content, higher intensity, and lower musical energy, as in Laurie Klein's "I Love You, Lord":

I love You, Lord, and I lift my voice
To worship You, O my soul rejoice!
Take joy, my King, in what You hear,
May it be a sweet, sweet sound in Your ear.

Moving into the next section of worship, it is assumed that there is sharing of the Word (read and/or preached), which can occur with or without other elements of worship. In liturgical settings, the Word section may also include creeds, confession and absolution, and prayers. Songs in this section can include songs those that express thankfulness, describe our brokenness and need for a Saviour, state our faith, and again, offer sung praise and prayer. Hanson's "Lord, Listen to Your Children" is useful in this portion of a worship time:

On bended knee with needy hearts we come and pray.
Lord, listen to your children.
With willing hearts and open arms, we come and pray.
Lord, listen to your children.
With simple words of heartfelt thanks we come.
Believing in your promises we come.
On bended knee with needy hearts we come and pray.
Lord, listen to your children, listen to your children.

Because this song is sung from the perspective of the community, its highest and best use comes before or after the prayers of the people, or intercessory prayers. Sung prayers and praise form the most intimate expression of worship, and are most appropriately found at or near the center of worship. Consider this chorus of individual prayer by Paul Baloche:

Open the eyes of my heart, Lord,
Open the eyes of my heart,
I want to see You, I want to see You.
To see You high and lifted up,
Shining in the light of Your glory;
Pour out Your pow'r and love
As we sing "holy, holy, holy."

During the Lord's Supper we have a wonderful opportunity for singing that embraces the profound symbolism of the actions embodied in this ritual. We also have an opportunity for singing that speaks our beliefs about what is actually happening during the Lord's Supper, and what God is doing in our midst. Communion is much more than a "Jesus and me" event, which many contemporary churches have allowed it to become. As a worship event, it is powerfully symbolic in its representation of the importance of the community. The church should not forget that the bread and wine are representative not only of the body and blood of Christ but also of the community. As many grapes are used for the wine, and many grains of wheat make up the loaf, so are we individually part of a greater whole, the body of Christ. Communion songs are best sung from the perspective of the community for this reason. Consider this lyric of "As Bread That Is Broken," by Paul Baloche and Claire Cloninger:

> Many hearts are hungry tonight,
> Many trapped in darkness, yearn for the light;
> So many who are far from home
> And many who are lost,
> O Lord, Your wounded children need the power of Your cross.
> As bread that is broken, use our lives,
> As wine that is poured out, a willing sacrifice;
> Empower us, Father, to share the love of Christ,
> As bread that is broken, Lord, use our lives.

What wonderful imagery embodies this song, and how perfect it is as a communion song! Not only does it allude to the community's role in the Lord's Supper, but it goes further by identifying what happens in the breaking of the bread and the sharing of the wine. They are portioned, and portioned they empower many. The wine and bread return to "many" once again, but return to many transformed, and in their transformation is their power.

The Lord's Supper is also a good time for a song sung from the perspective of God, which bears in the lyric God's own promises from Scripture. Handt Hanson's "Come to Me Today" does this beautifully:

My body's broken, my blood is given
For you, my children, as we share this day.
Your sins forgiven, your strength renewed
As you come to me today.
I know your sinning, I feel your hurting,
I want to make you new again.
Your search is over, I'm your creator,
I will change your life today.
As you come to me today, I will change your life today.
As you come to me today, I will change your life today.

Songs for the conclusion of the service may have several qualities. They can "nail the take-home" by referring once more to the theme of worship. If, for instance, the service focuses on themes of trusting God, a song such as my "Set Sail" would be an excellent sending song:

Set sail, into God's promises,
Set sail, into the light.
Set sail, though the skies may be stormy,
And the seas may be rough.
Set sail, with Christ beside you.
Set sail, his hand to guide you.
Set sail into God's love.

The ideal sending song is one sung from the perspective of the community. It celebrates. It recounts the worship theme. It empowers. It even blesses, as in the benediction-like "May You Run and Not Be Weary," sung by the community from the perspective of one person for the benefit of every other person at the conclusion of worship:

May you run and not be weary.
May your life be filled with song.
And may the love of God continue
To give you hope and keep you strong.
And may you run and not be weary.
May your life be filled with joy!
And may the road you travel always lead you home.

This song by Handt Hanson is a powerful symbol of benediction, as every person singing is both blessing and being blessed by every other person in the act of singing. Songs with "go" as keywords are also excellent as sending songs, as in this chorus of Graham Kendrick's "Go Forth in His Name":

Go forth in His name,
Proclaiming "Jesus reigns,"
Now is the time for the church to arise and proclaim Him,
"Jesus, Savior, Redeemer and Lord."

The best sending songs are generally not high-energy praise songs. Rather they are the ones that provide the perfect segue into leaving, going forth, and serving in a broken and hurting world.

Worship planners should also give careful consideration to the music chosen for other times in the worship service, such as the gathering of the offering or a baptism. The offering is used in many churches as a time for the special music, but rethinking this practice is encouraged. Songs of the community and its members' commitment of their lives to God and God's work are excellent as offering songs. Consider the Dwight Liles song "We Are An Offering":

We lift our voices, we lift our hands,
We lift our lives up to You, we are an offering;
Lord, use our voices, Lord, use our hands,
Lord, use our lives, they are Yours, we are an offering.
All that we have, all that we are,
All that we hope to be we give to You, we give to You.

Baptism is a worship event that calls for a special song sung by the community for celebrating with those being baptized and proclaiming the gift of new life. I wrote "In the Water" to recognize the gifts of baptism and to celebrate with the newly baptized the reality of belonging to a new family in baptism, with lyrics that spring from Luther's flood prayer:

In the beginning, God created life in the water.
Ever-sustaining, it is the gift of life for every living thing.
There is a blessing as we welcome you in the water.
Joining together here, Jesus is with us now,
There's a mysterious adoption here somehow,
In the water.
In the water, new life has been given,
In the water, we see Jesus risen,
In the water, the kingdom is come,
In this waterdeath real life has just begun.

The work sheet found in appendix E serves as a worship planning tool based on the fourfold pattern of worship described in this section. Each section includes reminders of which types of songs serve which worship functions. This work sheet is fairly exhaustive, and creativity within its structure is vital. Using every line of the chart would result in a service with too much music, so caution should be exercised in determining which worship functions will be supported with how much music from week to week. The worksheet can also be downloaded from the CD-ROM, and can be altered to suit varied needs.

New Worship and the Church Year and Lectionary

Planners of contemporary and alternative worship often seek to shed the old patterns and structures of traditional worship. However, I believe that the new worship forms may find themselves quite at home in the traditional context of the church year. Some may regard the cycle of the church year as a religious "trapping" superimposed upon the Christian faith unnecessarily. But beyond the religious character of the church year, profound and ancient sociological reasons explain why it *works* to shape the worship year as a circle.

The human experience has been connected to cycles as a way of explaining or understanding life. The ancients assigned the concept of recurring, cyclical patterns of darkness and light to their understanding of the days, seasons, and years; time was understood not as linear but as circular. Regular and ritual events were put in place in the cycle of the year by our earliest ancestors to mark the expected changes to their world. They created the earliest celebrations of the solstice rituals "less to congratulate the seasons than to propel them on,"[3] to help nature complete its expected course. The church year is the same kind of invention. Just as the ancient celebrations of the solstices kept celebrants in touch with the recurring drama of the seasons, providing reasons for what had happened and reassurances about what could be expected in each passage, the church year gives us the same kind of personal connection to the past and future, a path that leads us through a larger drama and a fuller understanding of our own faith experiences. It gives us a closer connection to the story that sealed our salvation and the events and people that shaped the basis for our faith.

The seasons of the church year lend themselves to emphasizing themes that acknowledge "special" times of the year and foster rich and fresh possibilities for Christian growth among the people. Even the "ordinary" time (the long season of Pentecost between Pentecost Sunday and Christ the King Sunday) has its special themes and key images. Recognizing and using the themes of the church year is a way of breaking up what might otherwise be seen as monotony or sameness in worship. Robin Leaver states, "The church year needs to be explored not only by theologians and preachers but also by church musicians."[4] There's good news—the contemporary worship music repertoire is full of exciting possibilities.

The focus on growing in our relationship with and faith in Christ during the season of Pentecost is a wonderful theme to accentuate with our worshipers. During one outdoor worship season at St. John (June through September), eight flags planted around the worship platform waved in different shades of green, fluttering with satin ribbons in every green imaginable. The summer theme song was my own "Come and Grow":

Called to grow, we are called to grow,
To turn toward the sunshine, to drink in the rain.
Called to grow, we are called to grow,
To bloom like a flower, to ripen as grain.
Come and grow, Jesus calls us,
Come and grow, hear Him say,
I will sow by my Spirit, come and grow.
Called to grow, we are called to grow,
To open our hearts to the Master's design,
Called to grow, we are called to grow,
We are the branches and Christ is the vine.

Similarly, our focus on the multilayered paradoxes of Advent brings a rich sense of mystery to new expressions of worship. Advent proclaims the promises fulfilled and yet to be fulfilled, the light in the midst of the darkness, our salvation complete and yet to be completed, the newness of life in the certainty of death. Contemporary and alternative worship has customarily sought to demystify the faith, on the assumption that mystery may drive people away. Yet the success of the New Age movement demonstrates that the presence and identification of mystery is good; mystery draws people to and beyond itself as we attempt to peer through the veils that surround it. Our human natures have us always seeking and yearning for that which fills the "God-shaped hole" in our lives (the quote is from a song by the rock group U-2). The Christian church hasn't cornered the market on mystery; it's everywhere we look. Why, then, should we dispel our mystery? Why do we consider making our seeker services bereft of the Lord's Supper, removing our greatest mystery? Acknowledging mystery and wrestling with it as worshipers and leaders is honest. It gives our visitors the sense that there is something "otherly" about this faith, something truly and functionally supernatural, something the human spirit ever yearns for and still can't quite grasp. Rich Mullins's "I See You" expresses these Advent themes beautifully as he paraphrases passages from Isaiah and the Psalms:

Lord, You're leading me with a cloud by day,
And then in the night, the glow of a burning flame.
And everywhere I go I see You.
Everywhere I go I see You.
Lord, You take my hand and You wash it clean,
I know the promised land is light years ahead of me.
And everywhere I go I see You.
And the eagle flies and the rivers run,
I look through the night, and I can see the rising Son,
And everywhere I go I see You.
Well, the grass will die, and the flowers fall,
But Your Word's alive, and it will be after all.
And everywhere I go I see You.

Lent, with its spiritual depth and focus on our brokenness and our need for a Saviour, gives the community a valuable opportunity to wade in the deeper waters of faith. Beyond simply rearranging our services and importing a contemporary Kyrie, we can echo the themes of traditional Lenten worship in contemporary and traditional services. We can forgo our alleluias and sing instead of captivity; we can confess our human frailties and our inability to fix them. We can echo the psalmist's lament in contemporary words. Consider having the congregation sing a contemporary, repackaged rendition of the traditional "By The Waters" in a round:

By the waters, the waters of Babylon
We lay down and wept, and wept for you, Zion.
We remember you, remember you, remember you, Zion.

The music need not be minor-key or dirgelike. The theme of Russell Fragar's "Show Me Your Ways" confesses our desire to walk with our God, but does so in a contemporary style:

Show me Your ways that I may walk with You,
Show me Your ways, I put my hope in You;
The cry of my heart is to love You more,
To live with the touch of Your hand,
Stronger each day, show me Your ways.

The church year can be successfully observed in contemporary and alternative worship, and the repertoire is large enough to support and illuminate the major church year themes. Imagine creating your own list of songs headed "Great Songs for Advent," or Pentecost, or Epiphany. These lists are not hard-and-fast. Songs bear themes appropriate for a season of the church year, but they need not be used only in that season. Many can also be useful in worship services year-round. Customized lists can and should be made in each worship community context, drawing from the keywords and key images of each season of the church year.

Many new songs for worship have more than one major theme and therefore are usable in more than one way. For example, see Rich Mullins's "I See You," printed above. It is a song of both proclamation and praise. In the verses, we sing of the security provided us in God's care, our inevitable safety in God's love despite the chaos and darkness around us. In the chorus, we address God directly with a statement of praise that indicates our sense of the divine omnipresence and God's creating and creative touch on everything of this world. It is sung from the perspective of the individual, not the community; therefore it is most useful at the center of our worship, as a song of personal praise, or as a transitional song from proclamation to praise or from community praise to individual praise. But its major themes are an excellent match for Advent themes, with the description of the paradoxes of light in the midst of darkness, life in the midst of death, and our salvation fulfilled and ultimately yet to be fulfilled.

Consider Hanson's "Christ is Risen":

Christ is risen, sing alleluia!
Christ is risen, sing alleluia!
Open wide, the door is standing.
From the grave new life is springing.
He was dead, now He's living!
Alleluia!

Purely a song of proclamation, this song is replete with Easter themes, and is set in an arrangement reminiscent of something mainstream artist Bruce Hornsby might have put together. How perfect for Easter Sunday or any Sunday of Eastertide. It brings back our alleluias and includes the call to join in as we sing. It tells that most basic of Good News—He lives. As a song of the community's proclamation, it can be useful at any time of the year, but its highest and best use will be to support the Easter event and the church's celebration of it.

I attended a service at a megachurch in my area in the weeks before Easter, and we sang "Crown Him with Many Crowns" at the beginning of worship. How strange that hymn seemed in advance of the celebration of the resurrection. It felt as if we'd "stolen the thunder" from the Easter service just a few weeks off. I contend that the song would be more powerful, liturgically and spiritually, sung on or after Easter. Singing it before Easter made the worship seem out of step, almost like seeing Christmas cards on the racks of the local Hallmark store just after the Fourth of July.

A lyrics-only examination of each song that has passed through the first three filters will yield all the information needed for determining a song's highest and best use in relation to the church year. Admittedly, some are so generic that they don't speak to any major theme of the church year, and they will be useful almost anytime. However, many *will* have themes that can support the observance of the church year with a lovely intentionality.

Many churches that offer alternatives to traditional worship will offer those alternatives in the same worship space. For some congregations, the traditional space has colored paraments adorning the table, pulpit and lectern. The same colors are also used for the stoles or copes worn by the clergy, and are often thematic in sanctuary banners. For regular churchgoers, it's no mystery that the color of the paraments reflects the church season, but often our new worshipers or visitors to the alternative service have no clue to what those paraments and their colors mean. Observing the church year in our song selection and teaching the themes of the church year through preaching, music, and worship expressions will result in a more interesting, richer worship experience and the inevitable maturation of new worshipers as they learn and move deeper into the faith.

Using the common lectionary, which is similar in many ways to observing the church year, is likewise beneficial for those planning contemporary and alternative worship. First, it creates a common bond to other churches and other worshipers in other places. Second, it prevents us from reverting to our favorite Scriptures or the pastor's favorite Scriptures as preaching and planning bases. Third, it forces us to develop a wide repertoire of songs for contemporary and alternative worship. I recently visited a mainstream Protestant church whose contemporary repertoire was a mere 42 songs. Each Sunday, they sing at least five or six of these. This makes for frequent repetition, and I venture a guess that such a small repertoire will eventually lead to boredom and stagnation. When we choose songs appropriate to a wide range of biblical themes and stories, our repertoire will be blessed with a depth and breadth of variety. In turn, our worship is blessed, our worshipers are blessed, and our God is blessed.

Using the common lectionary is a good ground-zero for worship planning. The lectionary keeps worship biblically based. The pastor can consider which themes from the passages will be the springboard for the preached Word, and lift up one or two themes as key. The worship team leader can then go to the repertoire and find a number of songs that fit those themes. For instance, preaching on the "I am the vine, you are the branches" passage from John, the pastor may emphasize the importance of being grafted to God's love and care in our lives. The worship team leader chooses "Now God Our Father," by Jim Mills and Kirk Dearman, for the community's praise:

Now God our Father, You are the potter;
We are the work of Your hands.
Mold us and make us, make us like Jesus;
We are the work of Your hands.
Be glorified, God of our lives; be glorified in us.

This song doesn't use the same agricultural analogy, but it restates our need to be shaped in God's caring hands. It says, "We understand that we need to submit to your design, Lord, and your plan and your shape for our lives are the only way we really want to live. We want to bear the fingerprints of our Maker."

Many songbooks and hymnals have a Scripture reference index, which can help worship planners to find songs that make a scriptural connection to the preaching themes. I also recommend that every song passed through the first three filters be minimally "exegeted." By this, I mean examining the song lyric, finding and determining keywords, locating those keywords in a concordance, and finding at least one closely related Scripture passage that supports the song. Worship team leaders can make and maintain a custom Scripture index for their own custom repertoire, and thereby have quick and easy access to thematically connected songs for ease of worship planning for theme-driven worship.

Even when a lectionary is not used, such a system of Scripture indexing is extremely useful. For instance, when a pastor plans to preach a sermon or sermon series on Bible readings outside the lectionary, the church's custom repertoire and Scripture bases for that repertoire will help make a more coherent and successful experience of worship planning and worship flow. Songs can be chosen that have a direct scriptural connection to the verses of the sermon text.

With all four filters at work, worshipers will ultimately benefit from the power of the song-selection process. The system works with the bare biblical mandate that when we worship, we worship in spirit and in truth. We open hearts and enable the work of the spirit by using the best melodies and lyrics, by using songs that reinforce our overall mission. We sing only the truth as we know and believe it, because we've done the work of scrutinizing the messages in our music. With this system of song selection, our songs for worship can do what we ask them to do. We ask that our music bear our proclamations, which God inspires; bear our praise, which God inhabits; and bear our prayers, which God hears. The system works to help us encounter God through the songs.

CHAPTER 6

The Role of the Worship Team Leader

The minister of music is not merely a good technician who produces nice noises at various points in the progress of worship.

–Robin Leaver[1]

A new role in ministry is taking shape today. The position of worship team leader is one that requires knowledge of the church's worship and liturgical heritage as well as musical expertise. It requires a committed faith walk with Jesus Christ and a loving heart. Excellence and diligence in communication skills are essential because the role of a worship team leader is based primarily on relationships. Those relationships become the springboard for a creative ministry that builds bridges between the roots of tradition and contemporary culture.

There is no generally agreed-on job description for a worship team leader. From congregation to congregation, the duties vary, depending on the community of faith, its history, and its denominational ties. To begin to enumerate the roles, I will describe a worship team leader from the perspectives of the worshiping assembly, the worship ensemble ("the band") and vocal teams, and the pastor and other church leaders.

To the congregation gathered for worship, the worship team leader appears as the person in charge of knitting the service together as a smooth-flowing experience of encounter with God and with each other. She (or he) opens the service and introduces the songs, giving verbal encouragement for praising God through song. He might weave prayers through an opening medley, provide an inspiring introduction to a song, or quote Scripture between songs as a way of deepening the sung praise experience. She is less of a song leader and more of a praise leader, singing the songs of worship "as though she really means it," because she *does mean it*. He leads the congregation in prayer—generally a spontaneous prayer of praise flowing out of one of the songs, choosing prayer themes that tie the preceding song to the next event in worship, whether it be confession, sharing of the peace, or the sermon. Most important, the congregation sees the effective worship team leader truly *worshiping* in spirit and truth, praising and giving thanks to God. When this happens, a comfort level is created among the worshiping assembly that lowers self-consciousness and assists in heartfelt worship. The worship team leader also closes the service after the pastor's benediction.

To the band and vocal teams, the worship team leader is also *their* leader. The role encompasses all areas of musical leadership and vision:

- Finding and choosing music.
- Making musical arrangements and charts for the band and vocal teams.
- Administering and using copyrighted material appropriately. (Contact CCLI at 1-800-234-2446 for more information about using copyrighted songs in your worship.)
- Conducting rehearsals with the band and vocal teams.
- Coaching the vocal teams in vocal technique.
- Appointing members of the band and vocal teams to solos and worship leadership when appropriate.
- "Counting in" the band to begin songs.
- Communicating nonverbally with the band and vocal teams regarding repeats, tags, or surprise endings.
- Finding and rehearsing other musicians from the congregation as substitutes and occasional add-ins.
- Settling disputes among band members on musical decisions.

The worship team leader is also the spiritual leader of the band and vocal teams, leading them in prayer, Bible study, and fellowship through their ministry together. These opportunities equip the musicians with greater understanding of the message of Christ, increasing the likelihood that they will see themselves as leaders in worship and servants of the worshiping congregation.

To the pastor (or pastors) and other church leaders (deacons, elders, music directors, council members, committee or team members, associates in ministry, and other lay leaders) the worship team leader is a colleague in ministry who shares their commitment to creating worship that celebrates our identities as children of a loving and merciful God. From sharing dreams to planning worship to the very actions of worship, the worship team leader is part of a network of leaders who have a relationship of mutual support and respect. As peers, they regularly meet together, pray together, enjoy each other's company away from work, and inform each other of current projects, new ideas, emerging problems or challenges, and hopes for improvements or upgrades in their areas of ministry responsibility. Their relationships also require that they be spiritually accountable to one another, sharing their faith journeys as brothers and sisters through Bible study, prayer, and a willingness to be in conversation about the challenges and blessings of a life of faith.

To the pastor especially, the worship team leader is a colleague who has an area of ministry expertise and responsibility to which he or she has been called. The worship team leader does her work faithfully, performing her duties as a leader in that area of ministry without being obligated to embrace ideas or perspectives on worship that might be held by other members of the worship team, including the pastor (who, theoretically, has vested that authority in the worship leader by virtue of his or her presence as a staff member). In some congregations (especially the small to medium-size one), the pastor who is used to doing everything has to let go of some decision-making and let the worship team leader become part of the worship planning. For congregations that fondly remember the old days of guitars on Wednesday nights with the youth group, the worship team leader can say no to songs from that old repertoire if they are not appropriate for the new worship expression. When a beloved deacon suggests to the worship team leader that this Sunday's worship ought to include a song that occupies a special place in his heart, the worship team leader possesses veto power and can, without flinching, exercise it if the song is not worthy for the task it is called to perform in worship. In turn, the worship team leader should be able to explain the decisions she makes with authority, and should be accountable to the whole team for those decisions.

From the outside looking in, these are some of the most readily observable roles filled by the worship team leader. These roles spring from a rich set of relationships that need to be prayerfully, carefully, and diligently tended by the worship team leader to serve the congregation faithfully. The worship team leader's primary relationships are with the triune God, the pastors, the volunteers, the worship assembly, and contemporary culture. These relationships will be unpacked in the remainder of this chapter. First, it's important to explore some basic principles that a worship team leader must consider essential for Christian worship.

Worship Principles for the Worship Team Leader

The guiding principle for the worship team leader is that nothing in the job description is more important than worship. Everything the worship team leader does is for the sake of worship. Morgenthaler says the church must in this respect be like David. "Worship was, unequivocally, number one in David's life."[2] It must also be number one for the church and for the worship leader. Hanson states, "Worship is the hub around which all things revolve, and we should be unapologetic about that. Worship simply shapes and reshapes everything we do."[3]

If worship is the centerpiece of congregational life, how shall we as leaders define it, or know it when we see it? How shall the worship team leader and his or her peers work together toward creating it? First, it is understood to be "the expression of our love for God, which Jesus said should involve all our heart, mind, and physical strength (Mark 12:30)."[4] Robert Webber states simply that "worship celebrates God's saving deed in Jesus Christ."[5] Morgenthaler goes on to say that "the most significant benefit of a worship service is connecting with God."[6] If our services "aren't transparent to the divine and people don't feel the presence of God, they will drift."[7] This reality requires that worship leaders also be familiar with principles of evangelism, because, as Morgenthaler states, "God is seeking worshipers. And God is seeking them from every tribe and every corner of the earth. The true goal of evangelism is to produce more and *better* worshipers [italics mine],"[8] worshipers committed and alive and excited in their faith. It seems a tall order to make evangelism a central task of the church, but it is not so daunting when the perspective is that "worship drives evangelism, and not vice-versa."[9] Worship that is created to serve the Gospel quite naturally serves the world. If it is created to serve the world, it may or may not serve the Gospel! When we serve the Gospel, we worship in spirit and in truth. When we make worship our church's number-one priority, and when we give honor to the only One who is worthy, we have a sound approach and a solid basis from which a worship team leader can be effective.

The Worship Team Leader and God

Without a vital, passionate relationship with Jesus Christ, a worship team leader might as well just give up and deliver pizzas. Even if she has exceptional musical talent and leadership savvy, if the inner light of Christ is absent, it will be evident in her ministry. The most important relationship a worship team leader can cultivate is with the Lord, and the most important action in that relationship is loving God with all of one's heart, soul, strength, and mind. Morgenthaler describes four essential elements of any relationship (and especially of a relationship with God) as nearness, knowledge, vulnerability, and interaction.[10] In a relationship with God, nearness is focusing on the reality of God's presence through praise and through the Word and sacraments. Knowledge is knowing who it is that one calls God, a God revealed through the Bible and through Jesus Christ. Vulnerability requires that one be open to God in prayer, acknowledging that we long to be known by God and yearn for authenticity and honesty in relationship with God. Interaction is synonymous with participation— doing something as a result of one's relationship with God.

The worship team leader who lives in such a personal relationship with God will infuse his or her worship leadership with the same quality as that personal relationship. This is the wonder of God's work in a human heart: that "those who would lead people into God's presence must be true worshipers, those whose first priority is . . . to minister to the heart of God."[11] It's essential that a worship team leader make a commitment to a daily quiet time with God that is well-balanced and formative of the faith necessary to lead a worshiping congregation. To make the most of that quiet time, the worship team leader should evaluate it regularly with this question: "Does my quiet time include elements of nearness, knowledge, vulnerability, and interaction with God?"

Discipline and spiritual maturity are also of primary importance in the worship team leader. Worship team leaders and worship teams "communicate their own personal devotion to God and facilitate a genuine sense of belonging, a 'we're all in this together' reality. Their eyes, facial expressions, and body language all say . . . 'I'm entering the presence of God, enjoying his love, forgiveness, and power. Please join me in this wonderful journey.' Discipled, committed worship teams lead by worshiping; they do not perform."[12] Eye contact is especially important to the process of leading worship. Eye contact communicates sincerity and spiritual contact. It makes a group experience more personal when eyes meet in the midst of praise. When we really *see* each other praising God, it empowers our praise and opens our hearts to true worship. Making eye contact means that music and lyrics are memorized, freeing the praise leader to connect with the worshipers. Memorizing is hard work, and many people balk at the idea. Yet the importance of spiritual connection with the people through eye contact subordinates that hard work to the ultimate goal of excellent leadership, which cannot be accomplished when a praise leader is staring down at a sheet of music.

Dutch-born priest and devotional writer Henri Nouwen captures the importance of spiritual maturity this way: "It is not enough for priests and ministers" (can we also assume worship team leaders?) "of the future to be moral people, well trained, eager to help their fellow humans, and able to respond creatively to the burning issues of their time. All of that is very valuable and important, but it is not the heart of Christian leadership. The central question is, are the leaders of the future truly men and women of God, people with an ardent desire to dwell in God's presence, to listen to God's voice, to look at God's beauty, to touch God's incarnate Word and to taste fully God's infinite goodness?"[13]

When worship team leaders can answer yes to that question and are centered in a relationship with the Lord, then their role in corporate worship points "beyond themselves to the God who transcends and transforms them."[14] As the worship team leader enters into corporate worship, the life of personal worship is translated into a medium through which God can move in the hearts of others. Ron Kenoly, a recording artist and worship leader at Jubilee Christian Center in San Jose, California, has stated, "If your purpose and goal is to be an example before the people of one who worships, of one who sincerely praises the Lord, the people who have a hunger of praise and worship will follow . . . just be an example . . . there are people who are going to enjoy that with you and follow along."[15] What seems most important is that "when we wholeheartedly give ourselves we are worshiping God with a right heart, a right spirit. When we do so in the context of the saving deed of Christ, we are worshiping God in truth."[16] This spirit- and-truth business is what seems to draw God's seal of approval. "God is seeking worshipers who will worship in spirit and in truth. But God not only seeks them, he fashions them . . . the Lord of the Universe can sculpt in us a living sacrifice that is holy and acceptable [Rom. 12:1]. All Go d asks is that we be willing."[17] Again, like David, we believe that God will draw people together in true communion through an authentic worship experience.

C. S. Lewis has written that "it is in the process of being worshiped that God communicates His presence to men."[18] Morgenthaler suggests, "Pastors and worship leaders, who we are as worshipers (or who we are not) *does* make a difference as to whether or not people sense God's presence."[19] One of the ultimate goals of the worship team leader is structuring the music of worship so that it brings people into the presence of God, recognizing that the average person in the pew is there with the expectation that "when we sing I want to encounter God."[20] Morgenthaler states that "a sense of God's supernatural presence is the first essential of real worship" and that this presence is what we crave when we come to worship.[21] Kenoly says, "When we openly display our love for the Lord, openly declare the goodness of the Lord, then that gives the opportunity for God to act on our behalf, for unbelievers to see how much joy and peace we have in our lives . . . they want that."[22] And there is no replacement for that authentic experience. "If we as leaders are not . . . giving God our sincere and heartfelt praise, no amount of perfunctory recitations, programmed enthusiasm, or stage technique will be able to manufacture God's presence."[23] Ron Kenoly has put it eloquently: "More than anything, I've just learned how to worship, and God has blessed that."[24]

The Worship Team Leader and the Pastor

Monty Kelso, a worship leader and seminar presenter, travels with Maranatha! worship workshops teaching about, among other things, the relationship between the pastor and the worship team leader. First and foremost, Kelso says, it is important that the pastor and worship team leader acknowledge who is the leader, and that the leader is the pastor. Kenoly supports this theory, stating, "Any church's worship style should be a reflection of the overall personality of the congregation and the pastor, the person that God has established over that group of people." He goes on to encourage the worship team leader to choose music that is going to "inspire those people and prepare their hearts and minds to receive the Word of the Lord from that pastor."[25] Equally important is that the pastor and worship team leader agree on philosophy and vision for the ministry of their community of faith. Reaching agreement on these important facets of ministry is the first task of the pastor and worship team leader.

Kelso urges the pastor and worship team leader to take care to define their expectations with one another to work together toward shared ministry goals. This work includes identifying the purpose of every service or event and determining an agreed-on ministry style. These tasks require the pastor and worship team leader to understand and agree on how any event or service fits into the congregation's vision, and together to define expected results, so that both pastor and worship leader can evaluate its success independently. As for ministry style, Kelso urges both pastor and worship team leader to understand what makes the other "tick"—that is, to endeavor to understand each other's learning styles, leadership styles, decision-making processes, particular gifts, and approaches to communication. He encourages them to evaluate their roles regularly, setting tasks aside and looking carefully together at responsibilities, measurable goals, progress made, setbacks, roadblocks, and priority needs. Kelso urges as most important that the pastor and worship team leader talk about these things together.

Next, Kelso recommends that the worship team leader and pastor invest in refining their relationship. Kenoly and Kelso are of the same mind in this regard; the relationship is based on encouragement, mutual support, and vision. The two leaders work as a team. Kenoly describes his relationship with the pastor at Jubilee Christian Center: "He sees me as someone who God brought there to help him do what he's doing, someone to help him realize the destiny of that church."[26] Kelso urges the pastor and worship team leader to develop oneness of mind—coming to agreement on major issues, agreeing to disagree on minor issues only, and knowing and respecting who has the ultimate "say." He underscores the importance of mutual respect. He advises the pastor to avoid these pitfalls: parenting the worship team leader, robbing him of the creative process, stealing the credit, destroying momentum by casual comments, and holding unrealistic expectations.

And the worship team leader, Kelso suggests, should avoid these snares: nagging the pastor, hoarding creative license, retreating to defensiveness, painting the pastor into a corner, and backbiting. Kelso reminds the pastor and worship team leader, "Don't forget to enjoy each other as people." He recommends talking, when appropriate, about personal issues such as successes, fears, failures, and discoveries. Discussing only the tasks at hand results in a narrower relationship. As an afterthought, he adds, "Be spontaneous enough to have fun."

Time sensitivity to one another's projects is important in respecting each other. Since so many responsibilities of the two leaders interface and overlap, being responsible to each other by meeting deadlines is essential to upholding the relationship.

Evaluation is the responsibility of both the pastor and the worship team leader. Each must ask, "Did the process of working together provide for a successful worship opportunity?" Kelso recommends measuring success in terms of spiritual fruit. Are people meeting Christ? Knowing God? Loving God? Obeying God? Serving God? Sharing stories and collected information is also helpful to track the results, and to see how the big-picture trends are fitting into the vision.

The Worship Team Leader and Volunteers

The worship leader works closely with many volunteers and groups of volunteers from the congregation, and for this reason the job is better described as worship *team* leader than just worship leader. Nurturing those relationships is a task best put first into God's hands through prayer, then acted out in the four elements of relationship described earlier—nearness, knowledge, vulnerability, and interaction. The worship team leader works with volunteer musicians in the band and vocal teams, sound and technical crews, and worship planning team members. The worship team leader's primary task in these relationships is equipping others for specific roles in worship leadership, both up-front and behind-the-scenes. Most important, the worship team leader helps the volunteer realize that volunteers have something special to offer in worship leadership, and that their gifts and talents are needed and appreciated. The worship team leader, like the pastor, is called to equip the saints.

Pastor, author, and radio host John MacArthur draws these pictures of the successful worship team leader from 2 Timothy 2:1-7. The successful worship team leader is a teacher and a farmer. In relationship with volunteers, she is most definitely a teacher—not only passing on information, songs, or skills to others, but also equipping others to teach and to pass on faithfully the same information, songs, or skills. The second picture is that of a farmer. The worship team leader strives to "grow" new worship leaders. The Holy Spirit does the plowing; the leader sows with the tools of musical rehearsals and new songs, Bible studies and prayer, planning meetings and new ideas. What is reaped is the enrichment of the kingdom of God as others realize their gifts and their calling to serve the body of Christ. In this way, worship involves people with the Saviour on a new and deeper level as the worship leadership comes *out of* the congregation, not *at* the congregation.

Worship for the new millennium is team-driven, not leader-driven. It is the worship team leader's duty to create and work with a worship planning team to ensure that worship is focused on Christ and the cross. It is the worship team leader's privilege to equip team members for and guide them in that task. Kelso describes the leader in this team relationship as a producer—one who "knows what we're shooting for" and has the resources to make that vision come to life. The worship team leader acts as a politician; he knows the process and represents the team in dealing with the pastor and council. The worship team leader acts as a pastor, helping volunteers become the people of God and grow in faith. She acts as a prompter, encouraging people to find and commit their gifts in service to God.[27]

The worship team leader designs the worship planning team and is the vision-bearer and maintainer of purpose for that team. He seeks team members who are passionate about worship and their relationship with Jesus Christ, who are thinkers, creators, critics, discerners, and observers "clued in" to the arts in general. Kelso encourages the worship team leader to know them well, to communicate clearly and specifically how they will contribute and the significance of their contributions; to combine socializing, fellowship, and work to keep the sessions positive and focused; to "go to the mat" on issues that matter; to expose them to fresh, new resources; to provide time to incubate new ideas before implementing them; and to honor their prior commitments.

Regular and generous praise for the contributions of the worship planning team members is equally important. Avoiding too much criticism (even when it is constructive) is essential for maintaining volunteer morale. Rick Muchow, songwriter and worship leader at Saddleback Church of Lake Forest, California, recommends this handy rule of thumb for working with musicians and other volunteers: "Three strokes for each poke."[28]

The Worship Team Leader and the Worship Assembly

Morgenthaler is clear in describing the worship team leader's central task in relationship with the congregation; "Our job is to make more and better worshipers."[29] This basic job description looks more complex when it's unpacked.

Mark Olsen, author and pastor, calls on the leader to *be a leader*, to be a bearer and communicator of the congregation's vision. "A leader with a clear understanding of what it means to lead the faithful community does not expect the followers to assert the vision for the community."[30] Rather, the leader "must first claim the specific vision of what God is calling the congregation to be" and then live out the vision through his or her ministry, realizing that "the congregation will only be as committed to the vision as their leaders are."[31] The worship team leader communicates that vision and leads the congregation into living the vision. He or she makes sure that the "congregation will be listened to and called to the mission of the church— to bring the world, all creation, in touch with God and God's love."[32]

A major criticism of alternative or contemporary worship is that it is a spectator event, driven by entertainment-minded, presentation-style leadership. This trap must be avoided by worship planners and leaders. Presentation-style worship requires nothing of the people, and those gathered for worship need not give anything of themselves back to God. To enable people to encounter God, Morgenthaler urges leaders simply to get out of the way. "We are responsible to . . . give people permission to interact with God according to His work in their own hearts."[33] Worship leader Tommy Coomes has put it this way: "God's highest desire is to have fellowship with us. As pastors and worship leaders, our job is to enable that, to make participants of our spectators."[34] Chuck Smith, Jr., writing in *Worship Leader* magazine, observes, "The more people participate, the more likely a part of them will open up to God."[35] Robert Webber has stated that worship "demands nothing less than the complete, conscious, and deliberate participation of the worshiper."[36] And it is pastors, worship team leaders, and worship planners who are "primarily responsible for the degree of interaction in your church's worship services."[37] The following thoughtful questions from *Worship Evangelism* will assist worship team leaders in increasing the participation level in worship:

1. What is one thing the people can do for themselves this week that we as a worship staff typically do for them?

2. In what small way can we encourage people to externalize what they feel internally?

3. What can we do to begin redistributing the "active worship space" so that worship becomes more of a "whole room" versus a "platform" activity?

4. As a worship staff, what is one thing we can do this week to become more "invisible"?

5. What combination of the arts can we try that will involve as many of the senses as possible?

6. What kind of interactive "twist" can we put on a standard worship activity (Scripture reading, prayer, etc.)?[38]

Music is perhaps the most powerful conveyor of the essence of the Gospel in worship. Church growth expert Lyle Schaller has stated, "[I]t is easier and more natural for people to worship with strong music support than to purport a more traditional approach."[39] "Music," he contends, "is the most influential factor in turning a collection of individuals into a sense of community."[40] In worship, "it is the most powerful thing we do."[41] As we've seen, *what* and *how* we sing are primarily the responsibility of the worship team leader with the support of the worship planning team. When done well and faithfully, this musical leadership becomes a gift to the congregation, a gift of the Holy Spirit, drawing the worship assembly into true worship through song.

The worship team leader is responsible for creating, maintaining, and evaluating an annual budget for music ministry that supports contemporary worship, and is accountable to the congregation through its appropriate board or committee for budget and financial concerns. This is no small task for many worship team leader-types, since the breed tends to be highly creative and "right-brained," possessing personality traits that make administrative and organizational tasks a challenge (to say the least). Cooperating with the systems in place for financial expenditures can seem wearisome, but must be attended to with care and forethought. The worship team leader should consider at least the following items when compiling an annual budget: equipment purchases and upgrades, equipment repair, music purchases, magazine subscriptions, CD and videotape allowances, software and MIDI packages, fees for professional musicians hired for special occasions, continuing education opportunities such as conferences or seminars, and mileage allowance for errands run on church business.

Once the budget is in place, it's up to the worship team leader to see that the money budgeted is spent. Ideally, budget support for contemporary worship should creep gently upward on an annual basis, but if budgeted monies are not spent, the congregation will quickly assume that the budget and expenditure lines for contemporary worship should stay flat or, worse, decline.

Worship team leaders have an internal call and commitment to the mission of bearing witness to God's reign. They also have an "external call from the congregation to be leaders."[42] As such, they have a responsibility to demonstrate "the dynamics of praise, righteousness, and compassion in their relationship with the congregation."[43] Olsen maintains that "God's people need leaders who, by their life and ministry, guide the community so that it can be faithful to its call."[44] He recommends that a worship leader live a "Sabbath lifestyle" that focuses on two actions—praise and re-creation. He states, "Leaders who practice a life-style of praise through prayer and worship are empowered to love both God and the congregation in an increasingly profound way."[45] It is also a lifestyle that embraces the biblical story, acknowledges failures, and dares to believe that God is still calling the leader to ministry. The other Sabbath characteristic is re-creation, or claiming time for play and laughter. "The ability to laugh, celebrate, play and live with imperfection are Sabbath characteristics" of re-creation.[46] Olsen urges worship team leaders to be open to newness, to "expect to be shaken and turned upside down so that they see life, the world, and themselves in new ways."[47] For the worship team leader, this is the dynamic of compassion, an important element in living out the Gospel before the congregation.

Olsen describes the dynamic of compassion as openness to that which is new or different, and he believes it "manifests itself in at least three ways for evangelical leaders: expectancy, learning, and vulnerability."[48] All are essential for maintaining a faithful relationship with the congregation as it worships and lives out its week-to-week ministry.

First, expectancy requires that worship team leaders "expect newness and change to continually break into their lives and their congregations."[49] An attitude of anticipation rather than dread is essential as changes roll through a community of faith, as well as trust that God is working through them.

Second, worship team leaders accept "the challenge to learn, to ever more intimately know God, the community of faith, and the world."[50] Growing as a person, as a Christian, and as a leader is crucial to maintaining a vital and effective ministry.

Third, worship team leaders need to be vulnerable. Olsen's theory is in harmony with Morgenthaler's: vulnerability is essential for relationships. Yet it is also the most difficult of these three qualities of compassion, Olsen says. It calls for courage, confidence, and faith. Vulnerability requires attention to "the voiceless and those who are different. The different ones may be members of the congregation or people encountered in daily life. They may be antagonists, voicing opposition. Compassion means that leaders are willing to hear the criticism of the antagonists, and to discern what, if anything, they have to say about God's activity in the leader's personal life."[51]

Vulnerability is also a key to avoiding another trap of the contemporary worship culture in which one person becomes the "community celebrity" and worship becomes centered on one person's charisma and gifts. No worship team leader should be enthroned on the community's collective pedestal, and vulnerability is the most effective tool for preventing this unhealthy dynamic.

The Worship Team Leader and Culture

Pastor, professor, and author Jann Fullenwieder has written about the Pentecost principle which the contemporary church embraces. She defines this principle as the freedom of inspired believers to speak a Gospel that translates into every tongue of every nation under heaven. This principle "commits the church to reading the culture and to translating the Gospel with a critically trained ear to all these ways humankind uses words. If such a wide array of tongues seems too vast to attend to, we must look again at the catholicity of Jesus. The very catholicity of Jesus impels us to find the words, in all their various forms, that tell of Christ in our time and place."[52]

This concept seems an important one for the church at a time when statistics tell us that fewer than three in ten people consider the church relevant.[53] What we in church leadership can draw from such figures is that either we are not reading the culture adequately, or we are not translating the Gospel understandably for it, or some of both. Indeed, the story of the risen Saviour is one that has stood the test of time and has been Good News for nearly 2,000 years. It is still Good News, yet fewer and fewer in our population agree that what the church does with it is worth their time.

Walt Kallestad, pastor at Community Church of Joy in Glendale, Arizona, understands the situation this way: "It's time to change or die."[54] His statement agrees with Morgenthaler's perspective. If we are going to take the Great Commission seriously, she believes, "we need to increase our ability to speak in the vernacular of our time."[55] Statistics suggest that "only 21 percent of all Americans would choose churches that offer an exclusive diet of traditional hymns. [Sixty-five] percent prefer churches that provide a mix of traditional and contemporary music (music that has been composed in the last 10 to 20 years.)"[560] This statistic imposes a significant need for change on many churches, if they desire to be something other than a religious club for members only. And for the worship team leader, this finding requires that he or she be very much in touch with the culture in which the church is ministering.

Hanson states unequivocally that "effective worship resonates with the culture in which it is found."[57] Morgenthaler says, "[O]nly that which somehow connects with the secular person's experience and knowledge base is going to be intelligible."[58] The trick for creating meaningful worship, it would seem, is to "enculturate the truth into the vernacular of a broken world."[59] Morgenthaler asserts that "the time has come to make technique the servant of spirit and truth."[60] These statements from many experts tell the worship team leader that it is critically important to package the message and symbols of the Gospel in a worship style that is accessible to anyone who walks through the door to the church. The leader had also better know a great deal about that secular, broken world from which they arrive.

Morgenthaler urges worship leaders to create worship "that dares to be a bridge, to acknowledge the seekers' culture by using their best stuff, not the trash. It incorporates their style of worship, their turn of a phrase, and their distinctive pattern of celebration, and it does so excellently."[61] Gordon Lathrop describes five critical principles worship team leaders can use for welcoming the elements of culture into the Christian assembly:

1. Is this a strong and real symbol or complex of symbols with a deep social resonance? Does it carry hope and human identity in its use?

2. Does it accord with the Christian doctrines of creation, sin and justification? Or, rather, can it be subverted to serve them?

3. Does it accord with the baptismal dignity of the people of God? Is it capable of being genuinely and graciously communal?

4. Set next to the biblical Word, does it illuminate God's gracious, saving purpose? Is it best exercised as a verbal symbol?

5. Can it serve and sing around the central signs of Christ, around Word and sacrament used especially on Sunday? With its use, are Word and sacrament still *central,* more clearly and locally *central?*[62]

With these principles in use, worship team leaders can acknowledge the culture, use the best the culture has to offer, and at the same time "transcend the culture with the whole Truth of Scripture and the Gospel."[63]

Authentic Worship

Above and beyond cultural relevance in worship is the importance of what Morgenthaler calls *real* worship. Real worship witnesses and "genuinely cares for people and offers a genuine relationship with a genuine God."[64] Real worship "provides opportunities for God and God's people to express their love for each other.[65] Morgenthaler contends that we have failed to make an impact on contemporary culture not because we have not been relevant enough, but because we have not been real enough, and that "cutting-edge relevance matters much less than being real: celebrating God's awesome and anointed presence, proclaiming Christ, responding to Christ's love, and being absolutely genuine in that response."[66] Going one step farther, it is indeed true that "if we are not real, we are irrelevant already."[67] It is important for the worship team leader to subjugate worship relevance to the goal of genuine worship, realizing that the average person in the pew is asking first, "Is God here? Will I sense the presence of the God of the universe?" and second, "Will I understand what's going on here?"

For the worship team leader, it is a worthy goal and a guiding principle to help that average person to answer "yes" to both questions.

A Call for the Creation of a Talent Pool

With the ministry role of worship team leader springing onto the scene for the first time in many churches, it should come as no surprise that there is no obvious talent pool for finding trained worship team leaders. Congregations generally must use "the great American know-who system" to find a worship leader. I hope that with this worship movement just revving up, we will soon see new training programs, opportunities, and resources for tomorrow's worship leaders, who are growing up with the movement today. It may be time for church colleges and seminaries to consider degree programs for training and mentoring contemporary worship leaders. It may be time for experienced worship leaders with the "baptism-by-fire" training that marked the beginning of the movement to come together as mentors of a new corps of worship leaders. The new generation can build on our body of knowledge and avoid the mistakes of the past. This collective wisdom needs to be pulled together to benefit those who will lead with us and after us.

How can the solitary worship team leader help create the resources desperately needed for this unique role in ministry to the church? I encourage them to connect with their counterparts in other churches, to come together and pool their collective wisdom. Share ideas, swap songs, tell horror stories, celebrate what works, fill in for each other when you're sick or away, borrow each other's musicians, visit each other's worship events, and create your own talent pool. Pray for each other, lift each other up, and encourage one another. Remind each other what a privilege it is to use the gifts of music to lead the praise of the faithful in worship of our Creator.

CHAPTER 7

The Band as Accompaniment and the Voice of the People

Praise precedes faith. First we sing, then we believe. The fundamental issue is not faith but sensitivity and praise, being ready for faith.

—Abraham Heschel[1]

The band accompanies the songs of worship chosen to carry the congregation's praise, prayer, and petitions. While I believe that great musicians are not essential for successful worship and great songs *are,* it remains that contemporary and alternative worship is defined in nearly all contexts as an ensemble-led worship experience. Therefore, the band is an integral part of how the songs for worship are made usable for a congregation. Whether small or large, composed of professionals or amateurs, and whether virtual or real-time, the band as accompaniment and leadership for contemporary and alternative worship is the most recognizable aspect of this new movement. Generally speaking, the organ—whether pipe organ or electronic—has no presence in "unblended" contemporary and alternative worship, and the instruments that support the voice of the people are guitars, drums, bass, and keyboards.

The complete ensemble for worship features an electronic keyboard instrument or a piano, acoustic or electric guitars, bass guitar, a drum kit, and a solo instrument such as violin, flute, or saxophone. A variety of hand percussion instruments is also essential for rounding out the sound. These might include congas, shakers, tambourine, claves, bells, and triangle. Most songs for contemporary and alternative worship will be keyboard-driven or guitar-driven, so these instruments especially must be played by someone with a high level of skill and expertise.

For baby-boomer worshipers (those born between 1946 and 1964), the favored keyboards for a band are digital or electric varieties. The use of synthesized sounds (available in either the on-board sound banks or in MIDI overlays) creates a musical opening that is inviting and familiar. Author, musician, and teacher Barry Liesch believes that people's musical preferences are formed during adolescence, and that those preferences drive musical tastes throughout life.[2] For boomers, these keyboard sounds drive and largely define the music of their generation's collective adolescence. The unobtrusive and gentle sound of the Fender Rhodes electric keyboard was especially present in the "ears" of that generation. Worship music designed for boomers can incorporate all the neatest sampled sounds of today's digital keyboards, including a variety of string sounds and the use of chorus and tremolo features.

However, at this writing, the cutting-edge keyboard instrument of choice is a grand piano, or other keyboard used as a grand piano substitute. Other types of acoustic pianos will work just fine, but some create line-of-sight problems. It's hard to see around or over some pianos, and that creates difficulties in communication between band members. If other keyboards must be used, a good piano sound from an electric or digital keyboard is absolutely essential. Synthesized sounds are becoming less and less favored. Worship leader and composer Dori Erwin Collins believes that calling on a trumpet player to join the band for a song is infinitely more appealing, and ultimately creates more authentic worship, than pushing a button and evoking a trumpet sound from the keyboard. For the worship setting, it is important that visual evidence of human craft be apparent in connection with what we hear. Asking the keyboard to sound like a trumpet, a flute, or a Hammond B-3 organ is the least-favored approach to worship music. According to Collins, the synthesizer is best used in combination with acoustic instruments. She urges congregations not to fall into the trap of assuming that "things with knobs are going to solve all your problems."[3]

In this era that caters to the tastes and preferences of "Generation X" and its distrust of institutions and leaders, the digital or electric keyboard has fallen out of favor. Synthesized music is perceived as less than honest among Generation X, and that perception has resulted in far less use of synthesized sounds from keyboards in mainstream pop music. It's hard not to agree with Generation X. Where possible, the use of an acoustic piano is the best choice for a worship ensemble. Support from a synthesizer is acceptable, if it is somewhat "back" in the sound mix. A simple string setting to serve as a "pad" to the music can warm up the ensemble sound without driving it.

Guitars are still central and essential to the worship ensemble. One or two acoustic guitars or acoustic and electric together can create a rich, lively sound for the ensemble. No more than two guitars are needed; in fact, with more than two, the ensemble sound will be skewed and the balance thrown off. A popular approach to using two guitars is having one played in the key as written, and the other transposed down to a lower key and "capoed up" so that both play in the same key but evoke a different arrangement of notes in the strummed or picked chords. The "capoed" guitar generally sounds higher than the other and brings a broader, livelier, almost mandolin-like musical quality to the guitar accompaniment.

Another popular technique for two guitars is the use of "Nashville tuning": one standard six-string guitar is restrung, using only the high octave of a set of strings for twelve-string guitar. When one guitar is strung in Nashville tuning and another in standard tuning, the result is a similar but more dramatic effect that broadens and enlivens the guitar sounds.

Bass guitar and drums make up the ensemble's rhythm core. The bass player and drummer have a close musical relationship and rely on each other, creating the basis for both rhythmic and harmonic elements. They should be close enough for easy eye contact or other signals, as they are in nearly constant musical communication. A full drum kit should be used only when the building is large enough to accommodate the sound without forcing the overamplification of all other instruments for an appropriate sound mix, or when they can be played skillfully and sensitively enough to mix in appropriately. Digital drums are another excellent alternative and are not unreasonably priced. The sounds are superb, and for a smaller room, the "mixability" of digital drums makes a full kit perfectly workable, as all volumes can be controlled at the mix board. Whether acoustic or digital drums are used, a variety of techniques should be explored to evoke the most from a drum kit, including playing with brushes, "Flix" (slender, matchstick-like pieces of wood bundled together to form sticks), and regular sticks, as well as making use of muting techniques. Other drums should be considered in smaller settings, such as congas, bongos, the African talking drum, and the Irish bodhran. These native drums can be used in larger settings as well, to add variety and interest to the rhythm section.

It is also desirable to have a variety of high-quality hand percussion instruments available, and to break down the perceptions of players and singers that hand percussion instruments belong only to the elementary school music classroom. When an ensemble remains mostly the same in all other instruments, the use of shakers, triangle, finger cymbals, bells, claves, and other such instruments can effectively lend an exciting variety to musical arrangements to keep all songs from sounding the same. I advocate the training and use of a hand percussion team, so that their skills and ensemble playing style can be available for the band and worship as needed.

By nature, a band sound is without melody. The accompaniment of an instrumental ensemble is nothing like the accompaniment of an organ, which almost always clearly articulates the melody. In ensemble-led music, the melody is generally absent, and must be provided by vocalists in leadership or by a solo instrument that highlights the melody, such as flute, violin, saxophone, or recorder. A musician who can improvise using one of these instruments is also valuable for lending creativity and artistry to songs. For example, during communion the congregation may sing a song all the way through, and then the soloist can play it to allow prayer, contemplation, and meditation by the worshipers, highlighting the melody or improvising within the song's harmonic structure. With solo instruments, it is important to vary what is offered so that it isn't always just the melody. Again, it is the worship team leader's job to employ people's talents artfully in the ensemble, so that every song doesn't ultimately sound the same in musical arrangement.

Unfortunately, the majority of congregations believe that they do not have the resources for a full ensemble such as the one described above. They wonder how they could manage contemporary or alternative worship without a wealth of musical talents and resources—not to mention the expense of a sound system to accommodate the requirements of band-led worship. Songwriter John Ylvisaker advocates using whatever resources the church has in its midst to create an ensemble. He ventures that the most outrageous instrumental combinations could be used effectively in leading alternative worship, believing that God has placed within each faith community that which it needs to move toward its calling and its mission.[4] If a congregation needed to begin with only a harp and a trombone, Ylvisaker believes God could work with them. Scott Weidler believes that all it takes (for any worship that includes music) is a pitch pipe. A human voice alone can effectively lead contemporary and alternative worship.[5] I agree! It's also important to realize that worship leadership need not be "spectacular." Music that is played well and prayerfully will be empowered and blessed to be a blessing. Well-rendered music also invites others, and an ensemble will likely grow out of even one person's faithful gift of musical talent used in leadership and invitation.

In the scenario described above, in which many churches lack sufficient musical or financial resources to undertake the ensemble approach to contemporary and alternative worship, some are tempted to follow an easy, known road, the highly advertised high-tech synthesized route, or to resort to the use of prerecorded "tracks" of instrumental accompaniments. Both require nothing more than pushing the play button and joining in. Although synthesized, sequenced tracks, MIDI packages, and recorded tracks are attractive, assure a professional sound, and are reasonably priced, these are not encouraged. Chiefly, they lack the element of visible human craft, they lack a vital interaction between people and leader, and they tell all who come through the doors that "we don't have anyone here good enough to lead us, and we haven't made it a priority to find anyone good enough to lead us, so we've put our leadership in a can."

The saddest result of using "canned" music is the inevitable impoverishment of the community. No new musicians rise up to join the ensemble, because there isn't an ensemble to join, and no mentoring of future worship leaders takes place. It is far better to use the human gifts of the congregation, even when they are humble, and to pray and speak the needs, waiting on God to raise the leaders and the talent to match the vision. Barry Liesch believes that where there is even one good musician, others will eventually and quite naturally join in. Better to allow one good musician to lead and invite others than to squelch the opportunity of ever growing a live ensemble by using professionally recorded and produced tracks.

Quentin Faulkner identifies a problem in the "mechanization" of the music of worship: The use of "drum machines, accompanimental sound tracks replacing live musical accompaniment, electronic amplification, electronically produced imitations of the sound of acoustical instruments, and the rise of recordings and tapes—all serving as substitutes for individual participation in the arts . . . has the unfortunate effect of inhibiting community singing . . . and transforming music into a vicarious, consumer-oriented, and nonparticipatory experience."[6] In this on-line era, it is important that people never feel that they could have worshiped just as well from the comfort of their computer terminal. Interaction and communication *between, with, and among people* will continue to be a basic human need, and the church must offer these in its worship and emulate this dynamic in its leadership.

Where a full band is not out of reach, Chuck Fromm, editor of *Worship Leader* magazine, cautions the church engaged in contemporary or alternative worship to avoid falling prey to what he calls "the pseudo-event effect."[7] Fromm defines the pseudo-event as one carefully crafted for satisfying the deep human need for a supernatural encounter. He explains that we live in a pseudo-event culture, where the safely controlled limit of the "spectacular" is safer than the real and authentic. "The heart of the pseudo-event is magic, not faith," he observes.[8] Yet he encourages the worship team leader to realize "that what people really need is to encounter God, not just sacred production . . . Faith moves the worshiper from being a mere 'religious tourist' on a magic-carpet ride to a traveler experiencing the richness, wonder and strength of God Most High."[9]

The temptation we face is to strive continually to create the spectacular, which draws attention to leadership, resources, and talent rather than to the grace of God and God's presence in our midst. Pseudo-event mentality creates tangential investments of interest, commitment, momentum, and energy in the "stuff" of worship rather than in worship itself. If we are faithful servants, we continually commit our musical resources to servanthood of the Gospel, carefully and regularly examining our goals and objectives in worship planning, allowing for the humble and the lowly, the *unspectacular*, also to carry the words, images, and metaphors of worship.

Sound Amplification Basics

I will not go into great detail about sound issues but rather highlight the basics and the essentials for amplifying the ensemble. Ensemble-led worship usually requires amplification, even in a relatively small building, and even if the ensemble is made up entirely of acoustic instruments. Because of the nature of the instruments, it is likely that one or more will be too quiet to be heard amid the ensemble sound, and that the song leaders' voices will not be heard above the instruments.

Amplification does not mean that everything becomes offensively loud; it means that we have the ability to manipulate the sound mix, pushing certain instruments, voices, or elements of the sound forward so that they are easier to hear, and pulling back others. Manipulable amplification helps to make the ensemble work well for worship and prevents it from developing a sound more appropriate to a concert setting. It keeps the lead guitar from overwhelming the mix; it keeps the bass from vibrating the windows. Most important, *it can put the human voice out front in the mix.* The most essential feature of ensemble-led worship is the human voice. It is the bearer of the lyric and the melody. It is uniquely personal. The voice is attached to the heart and soul of the singer. It alone has the power to minister *and* to lead in the context of worship. Everything else in the ensemble is present to make a faithful, personal, human contribution for the accompaniment and support of the human voice—the human voice in leadership and the human voice of the congregation. Therefore, the voice or voices are unmistakably foremost in the mix. If the lyrics cannot be discerned, everything else must be turned down, or the voices turned up, or both. That is the simple, solitary golden rule of music amplification for worship.

This golden rule can be followed easily enough when a "snake" channels all the sound signals to a part of the room where the sound can be heard, judged, and mixed. In such a setting, the mixed sound is then sent to the amplifiers and pushed out through the speakers. All sound then emanates from the speakers. When possible, Dori Collins chooses a more natural, ambient approach to amplified sound. Each player in her ensemble has an individual amplifier and a small "private" speaker. The piano is heard through one speaker; the guitar through one speaker, the electric guitar through another, and the bass through another. The result is a more lively, natural-sounding mix, one that more closely approximates the sound of unamplified instruments. However, it is less manipulable because the "whole band" sound is not being snaked to a central mixing board. Only the bass player can turn down the bass amp. If that instrument becomes too loud and the player doesn't know it or can't sense it, the mix continues to sound unbalanced until someone is able to signal the bass player to turn down his sound.

No matter how the sound is amplified, there remains a chronic problem in virtually every church situation I've encountered. There will always be people who complain that it's too loud, and there will always be people who complain that it's not loud enough. Precious few will go out of their way to say, "The sound was great today!" The worship team leader must invest time and energy in finding and training a group of people to run sound, and see to it that no one runs the board who doesn't know what he is doing. All "soundies" should be trained by someone whose technical skills and whose music *and worship* sensibilities can be trusted. There's a difference between the advice a Christian sound expert might give versus the advice you'll get from the sound expert for your neighbor's son's basement rock-and-roll band. The worship leader gives this trained group of people authority to call the shots during worship for all issues relating to sound.

One more thing to remember: Sound people are the least likely to be thanked by those in the congregation, since their job is mostly invisible to the worshipers. It is important that the soundies get regular and generous doses of appreciation from the staff, band, and singers.

Congregational Song: The Work of the People

Contemporary and alternative worship has contributed to a unique problem in churches today, especially those whose tradition embraces a spoken liturgy of any kind. Without the standard liturgy and its traditional chants, responses, and spoken words, the "work of the people" becomes almost exclusively its common song. In this worship setting, with its up-front leadership, amplified sound, and visual focus on the band, it is not surprising that the song of the people quietly dies, and a "sit back and enjoy the show" phenomenon takes over unless the leaders work intentionally against this dynamic. Today the church offering band-led contemporary and alternative worship does not have great singing in the congregation, although many of those who attend would say that they come because they prefer contemporary music to traditional. Barry Liesch warns that the people's song can be easily eroded. He encourages leaders to make sure that the people's song has priority over individual or group performers. "The congregation is the first and most important choir," Liesch says.[10]

Handt Hanson urges worship team leaders to make what he calls a "huge hole" in which the worshipers can sense that their voices make a significant contribution and fit into the mix of the band and vocal team singers. "Full participation in congregational singing is one of the primary goals of any worship event. . . . When all is said and done, the congregation should feel their vocal contribution to the worship is essential."[11] His "huge hole" approach is working. The people at Prince of Peace are singing their hearts out.

The congregation must know on a service-by-service basis that its collective voice contributes to the whole in an essential way. Robin Leaver states, "Where church music is performed in a way in which the voice of the total congregation is ignored . . . it has ceased to be 'Church' music."[12]

Hanson recommends that once per service, the band and vocal leaders completely drop out so that the congregation can hear itself and its contribution without the overriding volume level of the band and the amplified voices of the vocal team. This can be done in a variety of exciting ways. In an up-tempo song, the band can drop out during one or more "tours" through the chorus, perhaps leaving only native drums or shakers to carry the beat while the whole congregation sings and carries the energy of the song. The band comes back in to conclude the song, moving the energy and excitement level up a notch. In a more contemplative song, the band can drop out as the congregation finishes the song. The vocal team singers can put down their microphones and walk out into the congregation, joining their voices with those of the worshipers. Rounds are somewhat risky, and although some worship leaders advise against them, rounds can be sung nicely without band accompaniment if vocal leadership is strong. Having the vocal team singers lead sections of the congregation in an *a cappella* round can be an effective way of calling up the voice of the people. "Call-and-response" songs are also making an enormous comeback in the repertoire, and are structured to invite the congregation to "sing back" phrases "lined out" by the vocal leadership. Such "lining out" can become cumbersome if done too often; use call-and-response songs sparingly.

What is required to encourage relevant and authentic worship among the congregation is a band that knows it is not the "star" of the worship gathering. The band must operate on the understanding that the time of worship is about God, not the band. A band that knows it serves the community through its leadership, and that it points to God through its music, is one that will help create a vital song in the congregation and will equip the gathered believers and seekers for a deeper, closer walk with Christ. This is no small task, especially when one considers that a band is made up of musicians. Musicians live in an ego-oriented environment of performance, of practiced and perfected technique shown through playing style and personal flair, of the sheer fun and enjoyment of playing. Musicians are used to receiving both criticism and applause for their public performances. Only through spiritual maturity, prayer, and growth together in faith are musicians able to set aside these expectations and invite the Holy Spirit to work through their musicianship for the good of the worship moment and service to the gathered community.

One of the worship team leader's primary concerns, then, is the spiritual growth and well-being of members of the band and vocal teams. Regular opportunities for spiritual exploration, prayer, Bible study, general conversation, "catching up," and "cutting up" with one another must be made part of the routine. Not only does this routine help the musicians focus on contributing their talents to worship in spirit and in truth, but it also keeps the band members and singers growing together as brothers and sisters in Christ on a shared journey. Try fellowship centered on eating (coffee and doughnuts prior to rehearsal, dinner together with spouses, pizza after worship), listening to current Christian hits together before rehearsal, worshiping together at another church from time to time, catching a concert of a Christian band that comes through on tour, and making yearly retreats to rehearse and connect without the distractions of the daily grind. The payoff for a fellowship centered on caring for your ministry and caring for your friendship is enormous. "Where two or three come together in my name, there am I with them" (Matt. 18:20, NIV).

CHAPTER 8

The Special Music Controversy

If Bach continues to play this way, the organ will be ruined in two years or most of the congregation will be deaf.

—Member of the Arnstadt Council, employers of J. S. Bach[1]

The appropriateness of "special music" or anthems in worship is a lively, multifaceted issue as vital today as it was hundreds of years ago. Among the churches engaged in contemporary and alternative worship, there seems to be a black-and-white distinction between the two poles of this issue, with very little gray in between. Some churches have made it a priority to offer a weekly anthem, and others have not. At the practical level many considerations influence the decision of whether to provide special music, and underlying the practical considerations are theoretical reasons for the special-music controversy.

In the practical arena, the musicians in some churches find that getting a special-music offering to a quality level adequate for performance requires an inordinate amount of precious rehearsal time. For them, using or not using anthems is a decision based on the best use of available time and resources. For each rehearsal hour spent working on an anthem, perhaps five or six worship songs can be rehearsed. When a worship team leader is paid to serve only for a limited number of hours per week, the leader must use those hours wisely. Often, anthem material becomes a "time vampire," and therefore is not a priority.

In churches whose bands do offer anthems, the leadership, the congregation, and the worship team leader generally agree that it is important to free up enough time and resources to make special music feasible. Working on and delivering anthems has an effective and important "payoff" for the musicians, the congregation, and the integrity of worship. In rehearsing and performing special music, the band is allowed a little more artistic freedom and fun, and these songs make up the growing edge for the musicians. That's their payoff. The congregation's pay-off is similarly enjoyment. The special music is a "presentation" that requires nothing of the worshiper except listening, reflecting, and joining the moment. Like the sermon, it gives worshipers an entry point to some aspect of faith and provides raw material for spiritual growth. It is another manifestation of the lively Word. For the integrity of worship, an anthem done well can enhance the worship of the people, allowing a spiritual or emotional response to the Gospel that they might not have experienced otherwise. The anthem may effectively "set up" the sermon or reinforce it.

Theoretical arguments surrounding the use of special music are familiar to the church musician. They resonate with controversies that have persisted throughout church history. Principally, those opposed to special music contend that such a presentation casts the service into a realm more of entertainment than worship. Entertainment inevitably results in the exaltation of the performers, the exclusion of worshipers from the action, and the sidetracking of the rightful focus of worship—God. The "entertainment" moment also creates a practical problem for the congregation's response. "Do we applaud? If we do, will the band feel slighted if we don't applaud next week? Will the children's choir think they're no good if we don't clap for them, too? Then we must also clap for the drama team." Soon, all of this could result in nearly every action of worship requiring a perfunctory round of applause. For some churches engaged in contemporary and alternative worship, such frequent applause has become a reality.

Similarly, Barry Liesch points out that churches that feature anthems from their bands can create the impression among worshipers that the band and vocal teams have the highest priority in worship. The song of the people inevitably suffers when such an impression is conveyed to the worshiping assembly. "You can't expect to develop a strong singing church if you don't work at it and allow sufficient time for it. When we fill up the service with . . . special music to the point that we de-emphasize congregational response, we are teaching the people to be spectators."[2] Gordon Lathrop declares that when the music of worship is primarily and typically the powerful performance of a few experts, it essentially replicates the culture, "barring participation, accentuating the people's . . . passivity."[3] Lathrop encourages the creative development of music to serve the Christian community, but cautions against music that exalts the performer and silences the community. Music that has "no room for the whole assembly's voice . . . will have much difficulty serving the gathering." He continues, "[M]usic will have to *serve*, turning its power to evoke and to gather toward the needs of the people as they sing."[4]

Theorists in the "con" department also highlight the worst-case scenario, in which the special music is a less-than-inspiring offering that detracts from the worship of the people. Whether the band is having an off-day or the anthem wasn't sufficiently rehearsed, things can go wrong anywhere from now and then to nearly always. When they do, the musical offering compromises the integrity of worship and does nothing to help the worshiper engage with God. A poorly performed anthem can actually drive people away from the church.

Theorists in the "pro" camp believe that special music is especially beneficial for contemporary and alternative worship *for the sake of the seeker*. Because it does not require anything of the worshiper, it becomes an item of hospitality for the visitor and the seeker. We sometimes forget that our worship isn't just for "insiders." The anthem is an especially valuable worship moment for the outsider in our midst. Special music, performed well, can then come an "attractor" for the unchurched, appealing to the entry-level Christian. Carefully chosen, special music can also enhance the worship theme and offer spiritual openings for the gathered community.

The practical and theoretical considerations of whether to use special music are inconclusive for the church at large. It remains a context-based decision for each church, one that relies on available time, skill levels, and financial resources to supply adequate staff and staff support. For a specific congregation, prayerful consideration of what is best for the context and constant evaluation of special music's effectiveness in worship is required. Awareness of the controversies surrounding use of special music should remain a central pastoral concern of the worship team leader. Lathrop issues a challenging call to the worship team leader: "[W]hen musicians of the community are marked with the humility of the careful liturgical teacher," the assembly's song can be both communal and personal, "one voice and many voices, an expert musician and all the people, working together in lively polarity."[5]

CHAPTER 9

To Blend or Not to Blend

"How much more profound will our worship be when the Son of God leads His church in worship? Isn't it time for us to agree? Wouldn't it be worth the effort just to hear His voice in our midst and sing with Him?"

—Joseph Garlington, Sr.[1]

In these high-tech, rampantly individualistic, confusingly pluralistic times, it might be easy for us to assume that a well-staged, engaging, seamlessly flowing worship experience, combined with state-of-the-art sound and video supporting an all-pro, band-led contemporary worship scenario, defines the "cutting edge" in worship. I don't believe this to be the case, and this chapter sets out to describe a different kind of cutting edge.

The first step in finding a different cutting edge is to recognize the validity and importance of the contemporary worship movement and to understand the elements that contribute to its effectiveness and attractiveness. As a movement now in its second generation, it has proved its staying power and has asserted its influence in our current worship landscape. It is no secret that, since the late 1980s, the mainline denominations have lost membership at an alarming rate. In 1997 one United Methodist annual conference discussed gently euthanizing 300 churches, and statistics now show that 50 percent of churchgoers are attending 2 percent of the churches.[2] Church futurists predict that churches with a worship attendance under 300 on a Sunday morning are in serious trouble in the coming decade.[3] Yet Patrick Keifert argues that "growing congregations often draw visitors *and keep them* [italics mine] because of the contemporary music in their services."[4] Jack Hayford asserts the authenticity of the contemporary worship movement, stating, "[I]ts fruit has been tested and proven worthy in a sufficient number of situations to show we are not simply dealing with a fad."[5]

What makes contemporary and alternative worship *work*? Martyred German theologian Dietrich Bonhoeffer provides this insight: "The Church is the Church only when it exists for others."[6] Contemporary worship sets the Gospel message in the music, language, and metaphors of the "others" of the surrounding culture. British writer and Christian apologist G. K. Chesterton asserted, "For anything to be real, it must be local."[7] Across the spectrum, contemporary and alternative worship aims itself at this goal. In addition, Timothy Lull, president of Pacific Lutheran University, states that people are "hungry for the transcendent, for mystery."[8] Recent reports by the Luntz Research Poll indicate that 86 percent of people interviewed believe in God, and that the same number believe in heaven.[9] Contemporary worship brings the mystery of faith and the presence of God to the worshiper in words, actions, songs, and symbols that can provide "handles" for the apprehension of Christian transcendence and the Gospel mystery by even the least sophisticated worshiper and the "unchurched seeker."

The repertoire of contemporary worship music is attractive because it is basically user-friendly. This music is a "lighter" musical genre than the hymn and therefore helps balance out the musically and poetically dense hymn tradition. As music of the culture, it creates entry points for those who don't or can't respond to traditional hymnody. Donna Knowles of Nashville-based Cokesbury's music-publishing department observes, "When you see a church go from 50 to 1500 in worship in just a short time because they start using contemporary music, well, it speaks for itself."[10] Martin Seltz identifies similar strengths in the contemporary repertoire. He says that people can sing a contemporary worship song without concentrating as hard as they might in singing a hymn; they are freed up for heartier singing and greater involvement with the song. He also notes that it is easier to participate in these simpler songs during times of the worship service when it is difficult or awkward to hold a book or a worship folder, or when movement is required (such as standing in line for communion). Seltz also recognizes that the songs of the contemporary repertoire provide an opportunity for a greater involvement of the palette of human emotions. He says, "[T]he best contemporary worship songs are a genuine exploration of human emotion *and* Christian faith."[11]

The second step in finding a different cutting edge is to realize that edge is not defined only by the seductive qualities of the glitzy, attractive, and newly crafted. William Willimon, professor of Christian ministry at Duke University, cautions against worship that embraces the stuff of culture too completely as a medium for the message. He reminds us, "The point is not to speak the culture; the point is to change it."[12] Christ's message, and the church's translation of it, has always had a countercultural, subversive core. Pastor, professor, and musician Mark Bangert points out that for Christians, our "humanity is not centered in our individual agendas, but by what stands at the center of our assembly," which he identifies as Word, font, and table.[13] "Worship is to be revolutionary. It undermines us. Baptized into Christ, believers are a new humanity being refashioned by God into the image of Christ."[14] Gordon Lathrop echoes this concept, stating, "We only impoverish ourselves if we forget that ancient symbols such as the language and actions that have originally filled the meetings of all the churches are among the richest resources to us in our need. A community immersed in Bible and rite has powerful tools for seeing the world anew."[15] Yet he has words of caution for those who desire to lead and plan worship. "In liturgy, as in Christian theology, to say an old thing in the old way in a new situation is inevitably to distort its meaning. Authentic continuity requires responsible change."[16] We can draw insights from these words and find in them a new definition of the cutting edge. Here, in the sometimes razor-sharp zone of change, we find some important old things along with the new.

In our attempts to forge in our worship a relationship with the culture, the worship team leader needs to keep in mind that embracing the "culturally relevant" does not mean dumping the past and does not mean we become hostages to contemporary culture. According to Hanson, "We in mainline centrist traditions need to do what we can to highlight the sacramental nature of worship."[17] Professor and author Paul Bosch contends that "what is required of worship leaders and planners is simple, but difficult: judicious selection from among the riches—old and new—of the Christian tradition."[18]

As a worship team leader, it is best to build bridges between where we have been as a church, where we are, and where we are going. Many see today's church torn between the old worldview (objective, rational, conceptual, cognitive, religious) and a new worldview (subjective, nonrational, experiential, expressive, spiritual). Morgenthaler suggests that we as worship team leaders avoid the "old" and "new" aspects of the worldview and take a *biblical* approach, as the biblical perspective is "not riddled with these polarities. It is a totally balanced representation of the character of God, encompassing both spirit and truth, supernatural experience and propositional reality."[19]

"For he himself is our peace, who has made the two one and has destroyed the barrier, the dividing wall of hostility" (Ephes. 2:14, NIV). From a biblical worldview, we can, as worship team leaders, lovingly move our congregations from the familiar to the unfamiliar. In the realm of music for worship, Lathrop implies the existence of this balanced perspective as well, recognizing that "there is no one absolutely pure and godly music . . . commanded by God or required by the Church, by which alone we may sing ourselves into heaven."[20] Westermeyer echoes this reality by saying, "[T]wo truths are held in tension, this time the old and the new. If we are faithful, we will sing both old and new music."[21]

Drawing conclusions from all of the foregoing, I assert that *the cutting edge in worship is occupied by an approach that features the responsible and innovative use of the essentials of Christian worship, along with genuine and effective invitation.* Consequently, contemporary or alternative worship (or traditional worship, for that matter) that turns its back on any of the essentials of Christian worship (Word, font, table) or that operates in any paradigm of exclusivity is not representative of the cutting edge.

More accurately, the cutting edge will represent a blended variety of old and new expressions of worship centered on the core of Word, font, and table. Handt Hanson requires the music of Prince of Peace to be "deep, wide, high and long as well as old, new, used and borrowed."[22] The cutting edge of worship will be unambiguously centered on the reality of God's grace freely given and revealed to us in Jesus Christ. Worship at the cutting edge will welcome the stranger, using the best of what the culture has to offer in its effort to be hospitable and understandable. Keifert encourages the use of music that transforms the worship experience into a public rather than a private event, music that melds traditional theology with contemporary musical idioms and that creates "a bridge . . . over which the gospel can have free course."[23]

Robin Leaver encourages the church to consider worship in which traditional and contemporary resources inform and support one another. "An understanding of the doctrine of the church informs us that our worship cannot be exclusively in the past-tense *[we can also assume here that it cannot be exclusively present-tense].* The past needs to be actualized in the present and heard alongside the contemporary."[24] Leaver quotes

Richard Hillert: "A preoccupation with any one style . . . can inflict a passiveness into worship, relegating the art to the level of wall-to-wall music that no one listens to. Tradition is most meaningful when it is allowed to manifest itself in ever-renewing creative expression—when it is carefully balanced with innovation."[25] Leonard Sweet describes a correction to the "praise revolution" as the "need for postmodern Christians to be bimusical—to be able to express one's belief in more than one musical tradition, and to know a second musical language and tradition almost as well as one's own."[26]

Blended worship blends musical styles not so much to be all things to all people as to use the best of what the church has to offer from across time and across cultures. It is a matter of responsible, mature stewardship of the church's music that aims to raise up disciples. Marva Dawn states, "Our goal is that worship practices will form character so that believers respond to God with commitment, love, thought, and virtuous action. The scriptures make it clear that God wants his people not to just feel good, but to be good."[27] Similarly, musician, professor, and author Calvin Johannson argues that our music exists to assist and encourage the spiritual maturation of the believer.[28] David Wells, author of *God in the Wasteland*, identifies the fundamental problem of the evangelical church today as the perception that "God rests too inconsequentially upon the church. His truth is too distant, his grace is too ordinary, his judgment is too benign, his gospel is too easy and his Christ is too common."[29] A responsible blend of the best of old and new from across time and space meaningfully addresses this problem.

Sadly, however, blending musical styles in worship is easier said than done. It is easier to be "traditional" or "contemporary" and much harder to blend effectively. Blended worship is not for the spiritually immature Christian or faith community. Unfortunately, most local congregations are not populated by the spiritually mature; the music leaders and the "folks" must be equally willing to resist the entrenchment of the traditional, comfortable, and familiar, and be willing and open to change for the sake of the Gospel. If they are not, they are creating what will likely become, in a matter of time, a "hospice church."

In my own experience, I have been a part of some uplifting blended worship experiences in the context of synod events or nondenominational seminars in which most of the worshipers were clergy or lay leaders. Never has the singing been heartier, or the worship more beautifully and faithfully blended, than in the context of such events. We can probably assume a high level of spiritual maturity among the worshipers at these events, and it manifests itself in the welcome and embrace of the songs of many times and places. The African drum, the guitar, the pipe organ, and the soprano saxophone all have a voice in these worship events. The participants are willing to join the unfamiliar song of the Asian believer, the Native American believer, the African American believer, the Generation X believer. Yet at the level of the local congregation, attempting to blend worship as these large events are blended can result in angry worshipers who feel that their own special, favored "code" has been undermined or usurped by the intrusion of unwanted elements from a frighteningly unfamiliar sector of the culture or the world.

For worship leaders and planners, working toward blended worship is first and foremost a pastoral and disciple-making issue. Change of this (or any) kind brings grief, manifested at many levels as the congregation adjusts to even the smallest changes in the worship experience. The "mainlines" have perhaps the greatest challenge in creating blended worship, because mainline tradition has in some venues become equated with the "sacred" and therefore regarded as unchangeable. Author and lecturer Bill Easum might assert at this point that "sacred cows make gourmet burgers,"[30] yet reshaping the picture of tradition must be a process lovingly and carefully guided, not pushed through a violent and immediate process like "grinding."

Creating blended worship is the most faithful goal in worship that is right for the next millennium. In most cases, it will require a specific vision that the congregation fully supports and embraces, it will require prayer, and it will require cooperation between traditional and contemporary musicians, breaking down the walls and decompartmentalizing the worship of the people. Most of all, it will require sensitive leaders. The leaders continually gauge appropriate timing and the congregation's readiness as they guide responsible change toward true "blendedness." Eventually, "blended" as a description of our worship may disappear altogether, when we've moved from a perspective that this is how we *should* worship to a perspective that this is how we are *privileged* to worship. Then our worship will truly be a foretaste of the feast to come.

As Keifert has stated, bridges are built in blended worship. The bridges help nurture and create spiritual maturity in the congregation. Bridges are built between the young and the "experienced," between the church and the world, and between the past and the present, creating a healthier, more vital church. A church embracing blended worship calls its worshipers to a bigger Gospel, a fuller grace, a more overarching truth, and a more radical promise in Jesus' saving love for all. I believe it is in blended worship that our gracious God and the church's worship at the foot of Jesus' cross can become a brighter light and an irresistible salt for the world.

Assessing Theology

Theological Filter Worksheet

Song title _____

Publisher _____ Date evaluated _____

Name of collection _____

Type of source _____

Page number, track or other identifying feature _____

Key words _____

Theological Cons   **Failures**

(Check all that apply–if any cons appear, the song immediately fails.)

Images and statements in conflict with Bible   _____

Images and statements in conflict with confessions   _____ .

Questionable interpretation/paraphrase of Scripture   _____ .

Scripture linked to incompatible images   _____

Works righteousness   _____ .

Absence of Christian content   _____

Theological Pros	**Points**

(Score 5 points each for all that apply)

References and images rooted in Scripture   _____

    Scripture references _____

_____

Baptismal images, references, invitations   _____

Eucharistic images, references, invitations   _____

References to justification by faith   _____

References to the triune nature of God   _____

References to Christ's work on the cross   _____

References to our salvation due to Christ's
work on the cross   _____

Acknowledgment of our brokenness
and need for a Savior   _____

Lyrics bear the perspective of the community
(we/us), not just the individual (I/me)   _____

Others: _____

Total Pro Points   _____

(more than 10 points in this column passes the song)

Does the song use exclusive or archaic language?

If no, proceed.

If yes, can the language be changed with permission of the publisher?

Publisher _____

Name of representative _____

Telephone number _____

Date of conversation _____

Result: _____

"Extra Credit" Questions

Does the song use male pronouns for God?

Yes *(No change)*
No *(Add 10 points)*   _____

Does the song demonstrate multi- or cross-cultural awareness?

Yes *(Add 10 points)*   _____
No *(No change)*

Total Points   _____

This song *(circle one)*   **Passes**   **Fails**
                          (more than 10 points   (a con appears)
                              in pro column)

Music Preferences Survey

Preparation:

- Set date and time for church member survey (and rain date if necessary).
- Set date and time for surrounding community survey (and rain date if necessary).
- Recruit volunteers for both surveys.
- Photocopy music preferences surveys.
- Identify possible locations for surrounding community surveys.
- Obtain permission (if necessary) to do surveying at places of business.
- Design and order novelty buttons. (Buttons worn by volunteers identify them as legitimate to those they wish to survey.)
- Prepare simple paper bookmarks that have the church's address, phone number, and service times for those who might ask for information.
- Prepare a box with a slotted top for completed survey forms.

Materials:

- Clipboards for every volunteer and a stock of music preferences surveys.
- Permanent ink pens for every volunteer.
- Novelty buttons for every volunteer.
- Prepared paper bookmarks with church information for every volunteer.

Conducting the Survey

Gather volunteers at a central location for a brief training period prior to the survey event. Give volunteers their supplies—a button to be worn where it can easily be seen, a clipboard with plenty of music preference surveys, a pen, and a supply of bookmarks. Go over the survey form. Clear up any questions the volunteers may have about the form.

Role-play the script below with a volunteer, showing how to approach a person for the survey: S is surveyor, and P is person to be surveyed.

S: Excuse me, ma'am [sir], I'm with Our Local Church, and today we are gathering information on personal preferences in music. Do you mind if I take 30 seconds of your time to ask you three questions?

P: Sure, go ahead.
(You're in! Now just ask your questions, record the answers, and say "Thank you for your time, and have a great day" when you're finished. Put completed form in slot-top box.)

   OR

P: No, I really don't have time.
(Allow nonrespondent to go, and say, "Have a great day.")

Some people will ask questions. Give your volunteers permission to answer questions themselves. The bookmarks supplied should not be given out unless the person surveyed asks for more information about your church. Remember, this exercise is not about evangelism. It is solely for the purpose of gathering useful information.

Music Preferences Survey

What are three radio stations you've set on your car stereo's preset buttons?

What is your favorite kind of music?

Who are your favorite artists or bands?

Music Preferences Survey

What are three radio stations you've set on your car stereo's preset buttons?

What is your favorite kind of music?

Who are your favorite artists or bands?

Music Preferences Survey

What are three radio stations you've set on your car stereo's preset buttons?

What is your favorite kind of music?

Who are your favorite artists or bands?

Matching Our Music to Our Mission

LEADER'S PACKET

A Music Mission Statement Work Conference

A one-time, half-day work conference led by the worship team leader and designed for the participation of the song selection team for the purpose of creating a musical mission statement.

Preparation:

- Conduct music preference surveys (see appendix B, part 1).
- Evaluate the information gathered, identifying the three most popular musical genres for your communities. Keep this information private until step 5 of the music mission statement work conference.
- Set a date and invite the team members.
- Ask one member of the work conference to prepare a snack for the group.
- Decide when to serve your snack (depending on time of day).
- Make a copy of appendix B-Part 3, page one. Add the congregation's mission statement under step 1.
- Make enough copies of the prepared Participant's Packet so that each member of the team will have one.
- Prepare the room for the work conference.
- Prepare an opening prayer.

Materials:

- Participant's packets (appendix B, part 3)—enough for your group.
- Pencils.
- Overhead projector, blank transparency, and pen or
- Flip chart and marker or
- Chalkboard and chalk.
- Photocopier.

A Music Mission Statement Work Conference
LEADER'S PACKET

Opening Prayer

STEP 1

The worship team leader and the song selection team review the congregation's mission statement. Our mission statement is:

STEP 2

Drawing from as many themes as possible from the mission statement above, each member of the team is invited to work alone to complete the following preamble:
   We will shape our repertoire with songs that:

STEP 3

Gather in a group. Ask one member to collect the worksheets. Using an overhead projector, flip chart, or chalkboard, one member lists the suggestions made by all team members in step 2. Suggestions similar enough to be considered repeats are marked with a tick mark in the margin for each repeat. All suggestions are recorded without discussion. Work sheets are then returned to the team members.

STEP 4

As a group, discuss each suggestion as follows:

1. Does this suggestion reflect a theme in our mission statement, or is it outside the statement's scope?

2. If the suggestion is outside the scope of our mission statement, do we still need it as we consider song selection, or can it be discarded?

3. Can this suggestion serve as a faithful guide for us in song selection? Is it broad but not vague? Is it specific enough so that when considering whether or not a song matches our mission, we'll know a good fit when we see one?

4. Is this suggestion expressed well? How could the language of this suggestion be improved to better serve our purpose?

Agree, alter, or discard the suggestions as a group, according to the discussion in step 4, making changes as the discussion ensues. Remember, this is your music mission statement. After you've discussed the list, then consider a fifth question:

5. Is there anything essential to our worship that is missing from these suggestions? Look for the centrality of the Word and sacraments. Is the importance of these apparent or at least implied in your suggestions?

Ask one member to serve as secretary, recording the final copy of the group's list of suggestions that complete the preamble from step 2 (We will shape our repertoire with songs that:).

STEP 5

Using an overhead projector, flip chart, or chalkboard, share with the group
the results of the music preference survey:
    The music preferences of our community of faith and our surrounding
community are as follows:

  1.

  2.

  3.

Therefore, we can add the following to our music mission statement:

We will shape our repertoire with songs that can be presented to the
congregation in the musical genres of_____,
_____, and _____.

Have the secretary record this addition to the music mission statement.

STEP 6

Explain to the group that the congregation will not use these genres exclusively but will be open to novelties, other musical expressions that are familiar to our community and that connect us to Christians in other places and in other times. Each group member proceeds as follows:

1. Using the list below, put a star by the three genres that will shape our repertoire.

2. Circle the genres you believe would be familiar for many in our community.

3. Cross out the genres you believe are too unfamiliar for use or may be offensive in our community.

4. Don't mark the genres about which you have no opinion.

Rock genres
    Classic rock and roll
    Hard rock
    Heavy metal
    Grunge/punk rock
    Alternative rock
    Hip hop

New age

Country

Bluegrass

Classical
    Renaissance
    Baroque
    Classic
    Romantic

Traditional folk and ethnic genres
    Celtic
    Early American
    African
    Latin
    Reggae or Island
    Other traditional folk forms

Contemporary folk

Rhythm and blues
    Classic blues

Black gospel

Southern gospel

Rap

Inspirational

Middle of the road

Jazz

Pop genres
    Adult contemporary
    Light rock

Chant

Hymns

Big band (Swing)

Others:

STEP 7

Ask one member to be secretary. Each member reads the acceptable novelties on his or her list. Make a master list of all acceptable novelties. Each member reads the unacceptable novelties on his or her list. Make another master list of unacceptable novelties. Discuss, if necessary, the two lists and come to agreement on the two lists. The secretary incorporates the identified acceptable and unacceptable novelties into the music mission statement:

Acceptable novelties to vary and enhance our repertoire might include:

_____
_____
_____.

Unacceptable novelties are:

_____
_____
_____.

STEP 8

One member makes photocopies of the new music mission statement for each member of the team, and distributes them.

Special Thanks

Closing Prayer

Matching Our Music to Our Mission

PARTICIPANT'S PACKET

A Music Mission Statement Work Conference

The music preferences of our community of faith and our surrounding community are as follows:

Opening Prayer

STEP 1

Our mission statement is:

STEP 2

Drawing from as many themes as possible from the mission statement above, work alone to complete the following preamble:

We will shape our repertoire with songs that:

STEP 3

Information from Step 2 is collated.

STEP 4

As a group, discuss each suggestion as follows:

1   Does this suggestion reflect a theme present in our mission statement, or is it outside of the statement's scope?

2. If the suggestion is outside of the scope of our mission statement, do we still need it as we consider song selection, or can it be discarded?

3. Can this suggestion serve as a faithful guide for us in song selection? Is it broad but not vague? Is it specific enough so that when considering whether or not a song matches our mission, we'll know a good fit when we see one?

4. Is this suggestion expressed well? How could the language of this suggestion be improved to better serve our purpose?

After you've discussed the list, then consider a fifth question:

5. Is there anything essential to our worship that is missing in these suggestions? Look for the centrality of the Word and Sacraments. Is the importance of these apparent or at least implied in your suggestions?

Our Final List: We will shape our repertoire with songs that:

STEP 5

The music preferences of our community of faith and our surrounding community are as follows:

1.

2.

3.

Therefore, we can add the following to our music mission statement:

We will shape our repertoire with songs that can be presented to the congregation in the musical genres of _____,
_____, and _____.

STEP 6

1. Using the list below, put a star by the three genres that will shape our repertoire.

2. Circle the genres you believe would be familiar for many in our community.

3. Cross out the genres you believe are too unfamiliar for use or may be offensive in our community.

4. Don't mark the genres about which you have no opinion.

Rock genres
    Classic rock and roll
    Hard rock
    Heavy metal
    Grunge/punk rock
    Alternative rock
    Hip hop

New age

Country

Bluegrass

Classical
    Renaissance
    Baroque
    Classic
    Romantic

Traditional folk and ethnic genres
    Celtic
    Early American
    African
    Latin

Reggae or Island
Other traditional folk forms

Contemporary folk

Rhythm and blues
Classic blues

Black gospel

Southern gospel

Rap

Inspirational

Middle of the road

Jazz

Pop genres
Adult contemporary
Light rock

Chant

Hymns

Big band (Swing)

Others:

STEP 7

Acceptable novelties to vary and enhance our repertoire might include:

_____
_____
_____.

Unacceptable novelties are:

_____
_____
_____.

STEP 8

Receive our congregation's new music mission statement!

Special Thanks

Closing Prayer

Matching Our Music to Our Mission Worksheet

Matching Our Music to Our Mission Worksheet

Song Title	Publisher	Date Reviewed	Primary Tier
			Mission Match (Yes/No)

Please note: This worksheet appears as a one page form on the CD.

Secondary Tier			
Genre Match?	Genre Adaptable?	Usable Novelty? Can band do it?	Result (Pass/Fail)

Evaluating the Songwriting

Evaluating the Songwriting Work Sheet

Song title _____

Publisher _____ Date evaluated _____

Name of collection _____

Type of source _____

Page number, track or other identifying feature _____

Key words _____

Music Quality Evaluation	Point Value	Points Given
Does this song have an identifiable form?		
If yes, what is the form?	1 point	_____
Presence of a bridge, multiple verses or a ramp	3 points	_____
Does this song have a singable melody?		
Good phrase length	1 point	_____
Pattern and creative repetition	1 point	_____
Melodic climax	1 point	_____
Good range	2 points	_____

Predominantly stepwise voice leading	2 points	_____
Leaps match underlying harmony	2 points	_____

Does the song have interesting harmony?
Song has more than three chords (I, IV, & V)	2 points	_____
Song has harmonic predictability	1 point	_____
Song has pleasing harmonic surprises	2 points	_____
Harmony fits well with the melody	1 point	_____
Song has a built-in key change	1 point	_____

Does the song have interesting rhythm?
Song has some syncopation	1 point	_____
Melody works well with the rhythm	1 point	_____
Tempo is appropriate	1 point	_____

Does the song have an adequate accompaniment?
Accompaniment is more than just the voice lines	2 points	_____
Accompaniment does not embody the melody	2 points	_____

Total Points   _____

Lyric Quality Evaluation

Is the lyric innovative?
Lyric uses familiar contemporary images	2 points	_____
Lyric has clarity and gets to the point	2 points	_____
Lyric has little excess wordage	2 points	_____
Lyric creates a visual, aural and emotional image	5 points	_____
Lyric has a climax	2 points	_____
Lyric has innovative rhyme schemes	2 points	_____
Lyric is clearly in the vernacular of the people	1 point	_____
Lyric follows usual speech patterns	1 point	_____

Lyric is free from anachronism
    or archaic language   1 point   _____

Is the lyric well constructed?
    All words have correct accents in their
        marriage to the melody and rhythm   2 points   _____
    Lyric matches the musical ideas   2 points   _____

Whom does this song represent? It represents the voice of :

Us   Me   God   Other   *(circle one)*

    If the song represents "us"   2 points   _____

In its orientation to God, does the song:

Proclaim   Praise   Petition   Other   *(circle one)*

                        Total this Page   _____
                        Total Previous Pages   _____

                        Total Points   _____

This song   PASSES   FAILS   *(circle one)*

Plugging the Music into Our Worship Work Sheet

Plugging the Music into Our Worship Worksheet

Service Date _____   Liturgical Name _____

Worship Theme _____

Vocal Team _____   On Sound Board _____

Worship Function	Bulletin Tag	Suggested Song Purpose	Key
Gathering for Worship	Call to Worship	Song **we** sing about coming to worship or about theme	
	Gathering Songs	Song **we** sing about God	
		Song **we** sing about God	
	Songs of Praise	Song **we** sing to God	
		Song **we** sing to God	
Hearing the Word	Special Music	Restate Theme-Band or Solo	
	Response	Song **I or we** sing to God as people forgiven/loved/saved	
Giving Thanks	Offering	Song **we** sing to God offering ourselves/our gifts	
	Response	Song **I or we** sing to God in response to God's gifts to us	
God feeds us the Meal of Life	Communion Songs	Songs **we** sing to God and songs God sings to **us**	
Sending Forth	Closing Song	Song that sends us out as people renewed	

Please note: This worksheet appears as a one page form on the CD.

_____ Service Time _____

_____ Preaching Text _____

_____ CCLI# _____

Song Title	Page/Date Last Used	Scripture

List of Recordings

Recordings are listed in order of the corresponding identification number on the accompanying compact disc.

1. "He Is Exalted," from *Glorify Thy Name*, Integrity's Hosanna! Music, 1986.
2. "Shine, Jesus, Shine," from *Amazing Love*, Integrity's Hosanna! Music, 1990.
3. "Give Thanks," from *Prayers & Worship*, Forefront, 1995.
4. "My God Reigns," from *Let the River Flow*, Integrity's Hosanna! Music, 1996.
5. "Glorious God," from *Rivers of Joy*, Integrity's Hosanna! Music, 1995.
6. "All Things Work For Good," from *Fresh Fire*, PrairieSoul Music, 1995.
9. "Oh How He Loves You and Me," from *Prayers & Worship*, Forefront, 1995. © *1975 Word Music, Inc. All rights reserved. Used by permission.*
14. "Make My Life A Candle," from *Make My Life A Candle*, Changing Church, 1991.
15. "I Love You, Lord," from *Maranatha! Music Classics I*, Praise & Worship Series, 1995; "I Love You, Lord," from *Petra Praise 2: We Need Jesus*, Word, 1997. © *1978 House of Mercy Music (administered by Maranatha! Music, c/o The Copyright Company, Nashville, TN). All rights reserved. International copyright secured. Used by permission.*
16. "Prayer of St. Francis," from *Plum Branch*, Angel Toes Music, 1993.
18. "From The Ashes," from *Songs of the First Light*, Changing Church, 1996.

20. "There's A Song," from *Songs of the First Light*, Changing Church, 1996.
21. "Heal Me, Oh Lord," from *Healing*, Integrity Music's *Scripture Memory Songs*, 1992.

Note: Examples 7, 8, 10, 11, 12, 13, 17, 19, 22, 23, and 24 were written and performed by the author to show "bad" songwriting elements.

NOTES

Introduction

1. Quentin Faulkner, *Wiser Than Despair: The Evolution of Ideas on the Relationship of Music and the Christian Church* (Westport, Conn.: Greenwood Press, 1996), 204.

2. Handt Hanson, author's notes, conversation at "Changing Church for a Changing World" national conference, Prince of Peace Lutheran Church, Burnsville, Minn., May 14, 1997.

Chapter 1

1. Barbara J. Bloemink, *Georgia O'Keefe: Grand Canyon Suite* (New York: George Braziller in Association with Kemper Museum of Contemporary Art and Design, 1995), 10.

2. Leonard Sweet, author's notes, plenary session, "Changing Church" conference, Burnsville, Minn., May 14, 1997.

3. Timothy Wright, *Community of Joy: How to Create Contemporary Worship* (Nashville: Abingdon, 1994), 20.

4. Wright, *Community of Joy,* 47.

5. Paul Westermeyer, "What Music Should We Use in Worship?" *Open Questions in Worship 2* (Minneapolis: Augsburg Fortress, 1995), 8.

6. Westermeyer, "What Music," 13-14.

7. Westermeyer, "What Music," 11.

8. Gordon Lathrop, "A Contemporary Lutheran Approach to Worship and Culture: Sorting Out Critical Principles," *Worship and Culture in Dialogue,* Anita Stauffer, ed. (Geneva, Switzerland: Lutheran World Federation, 1994), 142.

Chapter 2

1. Lathrop, "Contemporary Lutheran Approach," 139.

2. Marva Dawn, *Reaching Out Without Dumbing Down: A Theology of Worship for the Turn of the Century* (Grand Rapids: Eerdmans, 1995), 170.

3. Robin A. Leaver, *The Theological Character of Music in Worship* (St. Louis: Concordia, 1989), 11.

4. Scott Weidler, interview with author, York, Pa., Sept. 28, 1996.

5. Dawn, *Reaching Out,* 171.

6. Leaver, *Theological Character,* 11.

7. Sally Morgenthaler, *Worship Evangelism* (Grand Rapids: Zondervan, 1995), 108.

8. Leaver, *Theological Character*, 8.

9. Leaver, *Theological Character*, 10.

10. Leaver, *Theological Character*, 15.

11. Leaver, *Theological Character*, 11.

12. Handt Hanson, *Worship Inside Out* (Burnsville, Minn.: Changing Church, 1995), 1.

13. Lathrop, "Contemporary Lutheran Approach," 143.

14. Lathrop, "Contemporary Lutheran Approach," 138.

15. Morgenthaler, *Worship Evangelism*, 137.

16. Reed Arvin, author's notes, workshop at the Academy of Gospel Music Arts, McLean Bible Church, McLean, Va., Oct. 11, 1996.

17. Martin Seltz, interview with author, York, Pa., Sept. 28, 1996.

18. Martin Seltz and Scott Weidler, interview with author, York, Pa., Sept. 28, 1996.

Chapter 3

1. Stephen R. Covey, *First Things First* (New York: Simon & Schuster, 1994), 103.

2. Covey, *First Things First*, 104.

3. Covey, *First Things First*, 79.

4. Covey, *First Things First*, 103.

5. Gordon Lathrop, *Holy Things: A Liturgical Theology* (Minneapolis: Fortress, 1993), 20.

6. Hanson, *Worship Inside Out*, 28.

7. Morgenthaler, *Worship Evangelism*, 128.

8. Lathrop, "Contemporary Lutheran Approach," 146.

Chapter 4

1. George S. Mocko, author's notes on Bishop Mocko's sermon preached at St. John Evangelical Lutheran Church, Columbia, Md., Jan. 26, 1997.

2. Jamshed Bharucha, interview for the Dana Alliance for Brain Initiatives audio program "Gray Matters: Music and the Brain," National Public Radio, 1998.

3. Bharucha, interview, as reported by interviewer Robert Rand.

4. Bharucha, interview, as reported by Rand.

Chapter 5

1. Robert E. Webber, *Worship Is a Verb* (Nashville: Star Song Publishing Group, 1992), 186.

2. Robert Webber, "Renew Your Worship!" workshop booklet (Wheaton: Renew Your Worship! Resources, 1996).

3. William Strauss and Neil Howe, *The Fourth Turning: An American Prophecy* (New York: Broadway Books, 1997), 29.

4. Leaver, *Theological Character*, 13.

Chapter 6

1. Leaver, *Theological Character*, 8.

2. Morgenthaler, *Worship Evangelism*, 38.

3. Hanson, "Alternative Worship Overview" at "Changing Church for a Changing

World" conference, Burnsville, Minn., April 1992; quoted in Morgenthaler, *Worship Evangelism,* 42.

4. Gerrit Gustafson, "Worship Evangelism," *Psalmist,* Feb/March 1991, 31; quoted in Morgenthaler, *Worship Evangelism,* 47.

5. Robert Webber, *Signs of Wonder: The Phenomenon of Convergence in Modern Liturgical and Charismatic Churches,* (Nashville: Abbot Martyn, 1992), 25; quoted in Morgenthaler, *Worship Evangelism,* 47.

6. Webber, *Signs of Wonder,* 23.

7. Chuck Lofy, taped presentation, "The Voices of Change," at "Changing Church for a Changing World" conference, Burnsville, Minn., April 1993; quoted in Morgenthaler, *Worship Evangelism,* 24.

8. Morgenthaler, *Worship Evangelism,* 39.

9. Morgenthaler, *Worship Evangelism,* 41.

10. Morgenthaler, *Worship Evangelism,* 96.

11. Morgenthaler, *Worship Evangelism,* 102.

12. Morgenthaler, *Worship Evangelism,* 238.

13. Henri Nouwen, *In the Name of Jesus: Reflections on Christian Leadership* (New York: Crossroad, 1993), 29-30; quoted in Morgenthaler, *Worship Evangelism,* 53.

14. Westermeyer, "What Music," 10.

15. Melissa Riddle, "Ron Kenoly's Heart for Worship," *Worship Leader,* July/August 1995, 32-33.

16. Morgenthaler, *Worship Evangelism,* 47.

17. Morgenthaler, *Worship Evangelism,* 31.

18. C. S. Lewis, *Reflections on the Psalms,* (New York: Harcourt, Brace, Jovanovich, 1958), 93; quoted in Morgenthaler, *Worship Evangelism,* 101.

19. Morgenthaler, *Worship Evangelism,* 31.

20. Dr. Randy Kennedy, notes taken by the author, "How To Make Music Minister," workshop presented at the 21st Annual Christian Artists' Seminar in the Rockies, Estes, Park, Colo., July 31, 1995..

21. Morgenthaler, *Worship Evangelism,* 97.

22. Riddle, "Ron Kenoly's Heart," 33.

23. Morgenthaler, *Worship Evangelism,* 102.

24. Riddle, "Ron Kenoly's Heart," 33.

25. Riddle, "Ron Kenoly's Heart," 32.

26. Riddle, "Ron Kenoly's Heart," 32

27. Monty Kelso, author's notes, "How To Build a Worship Planning Team," workshop at 21st Christian Artists' Seminar in the Rockies, Estes Park, Colo., Aug. 3, 1995.

28. Rick Muchow, author's notes, "More Than Music: Six Things Every Music Minister Should Know," workshop at Saddleback Church, Lake Forest, Calif., October 1997.

29. Morgenthaler, *Worship Evangelism,* 138.

30. Mark A. Olsen and Brian Burchfield, *An Evangelizing People* (Minneapolis: Augsburg Fortress, 1992), 47.

31. Olsen and Burchfield, *Evangelizing People,* 40.

32. Olsen and Burchfield, *Evangelizing People,* 48.

33. Morgenthaler, *Worship Evangelism,* 67.

34. Tommy Coomes, notes taken by Morgenthaler, Maranatha! Music Leaders' Workshop, Phoenix, Ariz., Oct. 23, 1993, quoted in Morgenthaler, *Worship Evangelism,* 49.

35. Chuck Smith, Jr., "Leading People to an Encounter with God," *Worship Leader,* August/September 1992, 50; quoted in Morgenthaler, *Worship Evangelism,* 118.

36. Morgenthaler, *Worship Evangelism,* 49.

37. Morgenthaler, *Worship Evangelism,* 118.

38. Morgenthaler, *Worship Evangelism,* 118.

39. Lyle Schaller, interview, "Lyle Schaller on the Contemporary Worship Movement," *Worship Leader,* July/August 1995, 35.

40. Schaller, interview, 35.

41. Schaller, interview, 44.

42. Olsen and Burchfield, *Evangelizing People,* 47.

43. Olsen and Burchfield, *Evangelizing People,* 47.

44. Olsen and Burchfield, *Evangelizing People,* 54.

45. Olsen and Burchfield, *Evangelizing People,* 51.

46. Olsen and Burchfield, *Evangelizing People,* 52.

47. Olsen and Burchfield, *Evangelizing People,* 53.

48. Olsen and Burchfield, *Evangelizing People,* 53.

49. Olsen and Burchfield, *Evangelizing People,* 53.

50. Olsen and Burchfield, *Evangelizing People,* 53.

51. Olsen and Burchfield, *Evangelizing People,* 53.

52. Jann Fullenwieder, "How Does the Liturgy Inclusively Share the Christian Faith?" *Open Questions in Worship 3* (Minneapolis, Augsburg Fortress, 1995), 23.

53. Morgenthaler, *Worship Evangelism,* 31.

54. Walther Kallestad, telephone interview with author, Dec. 12, 1995.

55. Morgenthaler, *Worship Evangelism,* 31.

56. George Barna, "The Dream Church," *Ministry Currents,* April-June 1992, 3; quoted in Morgenthaler, *Worship Evangelism,* 129.

57. Hanson, *Worship Inside Out,* 26.

58. Morgenthaler, *Worship Evangelism,* 128.

59. Morganthaler, *Worship Evangelism,* 128.

60. Morgenthaler, *Worship Evangelism,* 31.

61. Morganthaler, *Worship Evangelism,* 138.

62. Lathrop, "Contemporary Lutheran Approach," 143.

63. Morgenthaler, *Worship Evangelism,* 138.

64. Morgenthaler, *Worship Evangelism,* 30.

65. Morgenthaler, *Worship Evangelism,* 48.

66. Morgenthaler, *Worship Evangelism,* 139.

67. Morgenthaler, *Worship Evangelism,* 139.

Chapter 7

1. Abraham Heschel, *Who Is Man?* (Stanford: Stanford University Press, 1965), 116; quoted in Leonard Sweet, *Faithquakes* (Nashville: Abingdon, 1994), 67.

2. Barry Liesch, *The New Worship: Straight Talk on Music and the Church* (Grand Rapids: Baker Book House, 1996), 230.

3. Dori Erwin Collins, "Lutheran Worship and a 90s Sound," *Perspectives,* Vol. 9, January 1994, 7.

4. John Ylvisaker, workshop at First Evangelical Lutheran Church, Ellicott City, Md., 1992.

5. Scott Weidler, author's notes, "Worship Days '96—Welcome To Worship!" workshop, ELCA Division for Congregational Ministries and Augsburg Fortress, York, Pa., Sept. 28, 1996.

6. Quentin Faulkner, *Wiser Than Despair*, 194.

7. Chuck Fromm, "The Pseudo-Event Effect," *Worship Leader,* March/April 1997, 4.

8. Fromm, "Pseudo-Event Effect," 4.

9. Fromm, "Pseudo-Event Effect," 4.

10. Liesch, *The New Worship*, 100.

11. Hanson, *The Song Collections for Contemporary Worship* (Burnsville, Minn.: Changing Church, Inc.).

12. Leaver, *Theological Character*, 17.

Chapter 8

1. Barrymore Laurence Scherer provided the commentary containing this quote, which opened a segment on National Public Radio's "Performance Today," March 21, 1997.

2. Liesch, *The New Worship*, 100.

3. Lathrop, *Holy Things*, 124.

4. Gordon Lathrop, "What Are the Essentials of Christian Worship?" *Open Questions in Worship* (Minneapolis: Fortress, 1994), Vol. 1, 24.

5. Lathrop, *Holy Things,* 124.

Chapter 9

1. Joseph Garlington, Sr., "Sympathetic Vibrations," *Worship Leader,* May/June 1998, 18.

2. Sweet, author's notes taken at plenary address, "Changing Church for a Changing World" conference, Burnsville, Minn., May 14, 1997.

3. Author's notes at "Changing Church for a Changing World" conference, Burnsville, Minn., May 14-16, 1997

4. Patrick R. Keifert, *Welcoming the Stranger: A Public Theology of Worship and Evangelism* (Minneaplis: Fortress, 1992), 112.

4. Patneapolis: Fortress, 1992), 112.

5. Jack W. Hayford, *Worship His Majesty* (Waco: Word Books, 1987), 21; quoted in Liesch, *The New Worship*, 235.

6. Dietrich Bonhoeffer, quoted without reference in Sweet, *Faithquakes* (Nashville: Abingdon, 1994), 193.

7. G. K. Chesterton, quoted without reference in Sweet, *Faithquakes,* 180.

8. Timothy Lull, author's notes, closing address, Institute for Liturgical Studies, Valparaiso University, Valparaiso, Ind., April 10, 1997.

9. "What Does America Believe?" *George,* December 1996; quoted in "Reality Check," *Worship Leader,* March/April 1997, 9.

10. Donna Knowles, telephone interview with author, April 22, 1998.

11. Weidler and Seltz, interview with author.

12. William Willimon, "This Culture is Overrated," *Leadership: A Practical Journal for Church Leaders,* Winter 1997, 11.

13. David L. Miller, "Where Is the Center?" *The Lutheran*, January 1995, 11.

14. Miller, "Where Is the Center?," 11.

15. Lathrop, *Holy Things*, 5.

16. Lathrop, *Holy Things*, 5.

17. Hanson, *Worship Inside Out*, 18.

18. Paul Bosch, "Shall We Schedule a Menu of Worship Services?" *Open Questions in Worship 2*, (Minneapolis: Augsburg Fortress, 1995), 21.

19. Morgenthaler, *Worship Evangelism*, 67-68.

20. Gordon Lathrop, "A Contemporary Lutheran Approach to Worship and Culture: Sorting Out the Critical Principles," *Worship and Culture in Dialogue* (Geneva: Lutheran World Federation, 1994), 147.

21. Westermeyer, "What Music," 9.

22. Hanson, author's notes, "A New Song for the Changing Church" workshop, "Changing Church for a Changing World" conference, Burnsville, Minn., May 16, 1997.

23. Keifert, *Welcoming the Stranger,* 112.

24. Leaver, *Theological Character*, 17.

25. Richard Hillert, *Music in the Church Today: An Appraisal,* eds. Carl Halter and Carl Schalk (St. Louis: Concordia, 1978), 251-252; quoted in Leaver, *Theological Character,* 17.

26. Sweet, *Faithquakes,* 67.

27. Dawn, *Reaching Out,* 175.

28. Calvin M. Johannson, *Discipling Music Ministry* (Peabody, Mass.: Hendrickson Publishers, 1992), 59.

29. David Wells, *God in the Wasteland* (Grand Rapids: Eerdmans, 1994), 30; quoted in Dawn, *Reaching Out,* 166.

30. William Easum, *Sacred Cows Make Gourmet Burgers* (Nashville: Abingdon, 1995).

CREDITS

Print Permissions

"All Around Your Throne" by Lynn DeShazo and Ed Kerr is copyright © 1995 Integrity's Hosanna! Music/ASCAP. All rights reserved. International copyright secured. Used by permission.

"More Precious Than Silver" by Lynn DeShazo is copyright © 1982 Integrity's Hosanna! Music/ASCAP. All rights reserved. International copyright secured. Used by permission.

"Open the Eyes of My Heart" by Paul Baloche is copyright © 1997 Integrity's Hosanna! Music/ASCAP. All rights reserved. International copyright secured. Used by permission.

"Go Forth in His Name" by Graham Kendrick is copyright © 1990 Make Way Music (admin. in North, South and Central America by Integrity's Hosanna! Music)/ASCAP. All rights reserved. International copyright secured. Used by permission.

"Show Me Your Ways" by Russell Fragar is copyright © 1995 Russell Fragar/Hillsongs Australia (admin. in U.S. and Canada by Integrity's Hosanna! Music)/ASCAP. All rights reserved. International copyright secured. Used by permission.

"Come to the River of Life" by Don Moen and Claire Cloninger is copyright © 1995 Integrity's Hosanna! Music/ASCAP & Juniper Landing Music (admin. by Word Music) & Word Music (a div. of Word). All rights reserved. International copyright secured. Used by permission.

"As Bread That Is Broken" by Paul Baloche and Claire Cloninger is copyright © 1995 Integrity's Hosanna! Music/ASCAP & Juniper Landing Music (admin. by Word Music) & Word Music (a div. of Word). All rights reserved. International copyright secured. Used by permission.

"Leave Your Heart With Me," "We Love You," "Lord, Listen To Your Children," "Christ is Risen," and "Come To Me Today" by Handt Hanson are copyright © 1991 Prince of Peace Publishing/Changing Church Forum. All rights reserved. Used by permission.

"May You Run and Not Be Weary" and "Clap Your Hands" by Handt Hanson and Paul Murakami are copyright © 1991 Prince of Peace Publishing/Changing Church Forum. All rights reserved. Used by permission.

"Into the Life" by Terri Bocklund McLean is copyright © 1998 PrairieSoul Music, Inc. All rights reserved. Used by permission.

"In the Water" by Terri Bocklund McLean is copyright © 1996 PrairieSoul Music, Inc. All rights reserved. Used by permission.

"Set Sail" by Terri Bocklund McLean is copyright © 1997 PrairieSoul Music, Inc. All rights reserved. Used by permission.

"Cares Chorus" by Kelly Willard is copyright © 1978 Maranatha! Music (admin. by The Copyright Company, Nashville, TN). All rights reserved. International copyright secured. Used by permission.

"I Love You Lord" by Laurie Klein is copyright © 1978 House Of Mercy Music (admin. by Maranatha! Music c/o The Copyright Company, Nashville, TN). All rights reserved. International copyright secured. Used by permission.

"Come and Grow" by Terri Bocklund McLean is copyright © 1997 Abingdon Press (admin. by The Copyright Company, Nashville, TN). All rights reserved. International copyright secured. Used by permission.

"Now God Our Father" by Jim Mills and Kirk Dearman is copyright © 1989 Maranatha! Music (admin. by The Copyright Company, Nashville, TN). All rights reserved. International copyright secured. Used by permission.

"Great Is the Lord" by Michael W. Smith and Deborah D. Smith is copyright © 1982 Meadowgreen Music Company (ASCAP). All rights reserved. International copyright secured. Used by permission.

"We Bow Down" by Twila Paris is copyright © 1984 Singspiration Music (ASCAP) (admin. by Brentwood-Benson Music Publishing, Inc.). All rights reserved. Used by permission.

"We Are an Offering" by Dwight Liles is copyright © 1984 Word Music, Inc. All rights reserved. Used by permission.

"I See You" by Rich Mullins is copyright © 1991 BMG Songs, Inc. (ASCAP). All rights reserved. Used by permission.

The graphic on p. 62 entitled "The Worship Hourglass" is taken from *Worship Evangelism* by Sally Morgenthaler, copyright © 1995 by Sally Morgenthaler, and is used by permission of Zondervan Publishing House.

Recorded Permissions

CD-ROM/AUDIO CD INSTRUCTIONS

This edition of *New Harmonies* is packaged with a cross-platform CD-ROM which contains the following materials:
♦ Audio tracks of musical selections representing the different styles discussed in the book along with voice-over introductions;
♦ Downloadable data files containing all the forms from the book appendices;
♦ Adobe Acrobat Reader for reading the appendix files for both Macintosh and PC computers.

All of the files on the disk—both data and musical—are accessible by computers equipped with CD-ROM drives meeting the systems requirements listed below; the audio tracks also can be played by a stand-alone CD player. Please note that if you listen to this disk on a CD player, the data files will be on track #1 and the audio tracks will begin on track #2. In this situation, readers will notice that the musical cue numbers in the book will be off by one. If you listen to the audio tracks using your computer CD-ROM drive, the computer will compensate for the data files and start the audio tracks on track #1, matching the numerical cues in the book.

INSTRUCTIONS FOR INSTALLING ADOBE ACROBAT READER 4.0

Windows

System Requirements:
♦ i486 or Pentium processor-based personal computer
♦ Microsoft Windows 95, Windows 98, or Windows NT with Service Task 3 or later
♦ 8 MB of RAM on Windows 95 and Windows 98 (16 MB recommended)
♦ 10 MB of available hard disk space
♦ Additional 50 MB of hard disk space for Asian fonts (optional)

Installing and Uninstalling:
♦ Uninstall Acrobat Reader 3.x using the uninstaller available through the start menu (if necessary)
♦ Make sure you have at least 10 MB of available disk space
♦ Install Acrobat Reader 4.0 – ar 40eng.exe by following screen prompts
Note: If you uninstall Acrobat 3.x or Acrobat Reader 3.x after installing Acrobat Reader 4.0, you will need to reinstall Acrobat Reader 4.0 for it to work properly.

After installation is complete, double-click on any of the .pdf files to view the contents and print as desired

Macintosh

System Requirements:
♦ Apple Power Macintosh computer
♦ Apple System Software version 7.1.2 or later
♦ 4.5 MB of RAM available to Acrobat Reader (6.5 MB recommended)
♦ 8 MB of available hard disk space
♦ Additional 50 MB of hard disk space for Asian Fonts (optional)

Installing and uninstalling:
♦ Uninstall Acrobat Reader 3.x if desired.
♦ Make sure you have at least 10 MB of available disk space
♦ Double-click on the Acrobat Reader 4.0 installer and follow the screen prompts

After installation is complete, double-click on any of the .pdf files to view the contents and print as desired.